The Wit of the Spectator

The Wit of
The
SPECTATOR

Foreword by Wallace Arnold
Edited by Christopher Howse

C

CENTURY
LONDON · SYDNEY · AUCKLAND · JOHANNESBURG

First published in Great Britain 1989 by Century
An imprint of Century Hutchinson Ltd
Brookmount House, 62–65 Chandos Place, Covent Garden
London WC2N 4NW

Century Hutchinson Australia (Pty) Ltd
89–91 Albion Street, Surry Hills, New South Wales 2010
Australia

Century Hutchinson New Zealand Ltd
PO Box 40–086, 32–34 View Road, Glenfield, Auckland 10
New Zealand

Century Hutchinson South Africa (Pty) Ltd
PO Box 337, Bergvlei 2012
South Africa

Set in Garamond by Deltatype, Ellesmere Port

Printed and bound in Great Britain by
Mackays & Chatham Ltd, Chatham, Kent

British Library Cataloguing in Publication data
The wit of the Spectator
1. Humorous prose in English, 1945 – Anthologies
I. Howse, Christopher
828'.91407'08

ISBN 0 7126 2903 3

CONTENTS

Cartoons by Michael Heath and David Austin

FOREWORD

Tricky business, Humour. Happily, I have been endowed with that most agreeable of gifts, the ability to set the world a-roar with honest laughter. This, I admit in all modesty, sets me somewhat apart from most of my fellow *Spectator* contributors. Blessed though they may well be in other virtues – research, computer technology, versification, what you will – they are blind to the nuances of humour. How often have my dinner parties suffered the interruption of the familiar 'tring-tring' of the telephone (dread instrument), upon the other end of which is a distraught fellow contributor, quite desperate for a humorous twist *à la Arnold* to an otherwise drear piece! Of course, I oblige. I shouldn't, I know I shouldn't, but I do. 'My dear Bron' I will say, should the contributor's name be Bron, 'Too earnest! Too earnest! Lighten the load for poor Joe Public!' Needless to say, my advice is always heeded – though rarely acknowledged! – and I thus find it most gratifying as I peruse the pages of this estimable tome to note that a very high proportion of what is termed 'The Wit of The Spectator' is in fact 'The Wit of Wallace Arnold'. Appropriate, you might well think, that the man who has been so often called 'The Maestro of Mirth' should now be introducing a collection of Hilarious Hoots which, but for the odd duff word, is penned entirely by himself!

Let no-one tell you that humour comes naturally to Wallace Arnold. In all my twenty-one years as Motoring Correspondent for *Punch* magazine, I worked at each joke until way into the night, polishing, honing, cutting, rephrasing, and then honing some more. Then – and only then – would I submit the finished manuscript to Uncle Bill Davis. Suffice it to say that after reading just a line or two of Arnold's Famous Aphorisms –e.g. 'Never embark upon any lengthy vehicular journey without first ascertaining that the aforesaid vehicle is in possession of that most useful of contraptions – a steering wheel!!!' – old Davis, no mean jester himself, was laughing fit to bust. A fellow professional tickler of ribs, he would have known, through his tears of unabashed merriment, that such 'bon-bons' are not created for the amusement of The Great British Public without a great deal of sheer, hard slog. Humour, you might say, is no laughing matter!!!

What, then, is wit? There are tomes aplenty on the subject – mostly, I regret to say, penned by po-faced boffins of a Germanic disposition! – but none of 'em, I venture, will answer that eternal question with the Chuckle Quotient of the pieces you are about to skip through. The inimitable Kingsley Amis on 'Sod the Public' (!), that king of the Tickle-stick, Mr Charles Moore, on 'It's a Funny Old World – Reflections on the Potty World of Politics', Miss (Ms!) Libby Purves on 'A Sideways Look at Baby-Rearing', A.N. Wilson on 'Doctor, There's a Fly in my Engine!' and that Pulcinello of the Public Bar, Mr Jeff Bernard, on 'Make Mine a Crumpet!' – a veritable galaxy of comic talent awaits you beyond these pages.

A word or two to those who wish to try their hand at the witty article. Bend back yer lug-'oles, me hearties, as me old auntie used to say! I believe all *Spectator* contributors are agreed that a prime giggle-inducer in this oft hilarious world in which we live is the chap who has a name appropriate to his profession. I feel those old ribs being tickled something awful when I hear of a Mr Albert Broom, who is a road-sweeper (!) in Cheshire, or Mrs E. Carr of Reading, who is – I kid you not! – a driving instructor, or Mr Cheese of Chippenham, who owns a record shop. A record shop? I hear you ask – but what on earth is funny about that? Fair question. But when I tell you that Mr Cheese's record shop is only two doors away from a general store which used to sell, among other things, yes, you've got it, cheese (!) until they decided to do away with the dairy counter in favour of refrigerated products, well, then I think you will understand why I am chuckling out loud. I also hold a soft spot for Mrs Shoe from Birmingham who informs me that she has drawn no end of smiles when signing her name on cheques on her visits to *shoe* shops!!

Another tip. I am a great one for the ingenious, mirth-filled names allotted to our Friends on the Left by our leading newspaper humorists. Who can forebear to grin at such creations as Fred Nitwit, General Secretary of the Union of Allied Nosepickers, or Alf Getstuffed, anti-apartheid rabble-rouser! Such names encompass sharp, highly sophisticated political rapier-thrusts while affording anyone with a halfway-decent sense of humour the additional bonus of an out-and-out belly laugh. Of course, our Friends on the Left may splutter with rage at such tweaking of their lofty ideals, but then a sense of humour has never been high on the list of priorities of Sid Socialist, alas.

Finally, it is the gentle perambulation through the lighter side of life that I have always found most appealing. There could be few prospects more enticing that 3,000 words by a good, old-fashioned, English (regrettably, Americans have little sense of irony) humorist on 'A Slacker's Guide to Lazy Gardening' or 'If It's Wednesday, It must Be Rome – An Irreverent Glance at the Package Tour'. Such delightful reveries teach us that humour need not be hurtful or – dread word! – satirical to make its points. Far from it: chuckles spring aplenty from a pleasant totter through our topsy-turvy world, as Mr Grass, a florist from Totnes, presumably needs no reminding!

Wallace Arnold
London-Firenze-Dordogne-Morocco
January-May 1989

INTRODUCTION

A Scottish friend was explaining to me about the off-licence chain, Agnews, which advertised the competitiveness of its prices with the slogan, 'You'll always get change at Agnews.' Her father had once been seriously ill in hospital, and there was little chance of his recovery. Every time she telephoned to ask his condition, she got the same answer, 'No change.' Eventually she retorted, on the spur of the moment, 'Have you tried Agnews?'

Not a terribly funny joke, perhaps, though it made me laugh, but it illustrates something of what the humour of *The Spectator* is about. It arises for the most part from incidents in life which may be far from amusing in some aspects. When Ludovic Kennedy went to have some growths removed from his lower bowel, his consultant was joined by a visitor from Egypt. ' "You don't have many polyps in Egypt, do you?" asked the doctor, and the man from Cairo said, "Not in the colon," though without saying where they did have them.' Or take this incident from the life of a friend of Jeffrey Bernard's:

> Keith woke up one day sitting in pitch darkness. He groped around for a while and realised slowly that he was in a cinema. Further groping got him to the exit door and he eventually got out onto the street. He didn't know what town he was in but made his way to a pub where, with great embarrassment, he asked the barman where he was. 'Dover,' he was told. Then it all came back to him. 'Christ almighty,' he said. 'I got married yesterday.'

That story convinces and amuses with a strange echo of the great classical scholar Porson suddenly remembering in the middle of a session in a cider cellar one night that he had married that morning. If it happened to you it would be tragic; but there is a funny side to it. It is the same as one of the platitudes that some of my friends enjoy collecting and swapping: 'You can't help laughing, can you?' To which the answer is all too easily, Yes.

I would like to think that the pages that follow have something in common with the original *Spectator* of Addison and Steele (with which the present magazine, having been founded only in 1828, has no connection, save in spirit). In *The Spectator* No. 1 for Thursday 1 March 1710/11, Mr Spectator introduces himself:

> There is no place of general resort wherein I do not often make my appearance: sometimes I am seen thrusting my head into a round of politicians at Will's, and listening with great attention to the narratives that are made in those little circular audiences; sometimes I smoke a pipe at Child's [the resort of clergymen] and, while I seem attentive to nothing but the Postman, overhear the conversation of every table in the room. I appear on Sunday nights at St James's coffee-house, and sometimes join the little committee of politics in the inner room, as one who comes to hear and improve. My face is likewise very well known at the Grecian, the Cocoa Tree and in the theatres both of Drury Lane and the Haymarket. . . . Thus I live in the world rather as a Spectator of mankind, than as one of the species.

P. J. Kavanagh, with his poet's ear, could be Mr Spectator himself, or Swift from the pages of *Polite Conversation*, when he listens in at a strange pub:

> 'Evening Terence.' A Regular had entered. 'The usual?'
> 'You wouldn't try to flog me a pint of that Director's, would you?'
> Terence appeared an aggressive regular. The barmaid did not respond, drew his pint and said mildly: 'I went to see Billy Graham the other night.'
> 'Christ!' said Terence.
> 'That's what he said.' (This was getting good.)
> 'Typical Yank,' he said.

One step away is Ursula Buchan's fantasia on *Gardener's Question Time*:

> 'I was having an argument with my neighbour over the fence last night. He is adamant that Canadian pondweed, *Elodea canadensis*, is an example of agamospermic reproduction. I maintain it is just good, old-fashioned apomixis. Surely it couldn't be cleistogamy, could it? What do you think?' – D.B., Durham.
> 'It all depends on what you mean by agamospermy.'

Norman Stone turns Mr Spectator's technique on its head by

revealing the contents of the diary of an English colonel in Poland during 1919 and 1920. The diarist thought he was showing how quaint foreigners were:

At the Czechoslovak border 'a rude official attempted to turn us out of the train as we had not got a visé [sic] for his rotten country. . . . We were firm and told him that there were now so many small states to think of that this had been forgotten when visés were obtained.'

It is not that Mr Spectator does not care. Kingsley Amis, for example, in his catalogue of customer abuse, on the theme of 'Sod the public' seems to care so much that he is in danger of exploding:

MAGAZINES: The growing practice of not numbering advertisement pages, and so forcing the reader to turn through them while looking for what he wants, supposedly makes him more likely to buy and demonstrably sods him at the same time. . . .

NEW BIBLE AND PRAYERBOOK: A big one, sodding congregation, Church and people at a single stroke. Nobody except those in the trade wanted it.

The campaigns that *The Spectator* has waged recently, against the destruction of telephone boxes (indeed the whole telephone system), good architecture or the liturgy of the Church of England were foreshadowed by John Betjeman in his City and Suburban column during the 1950s. (He was later to be the first Piloti in the *Private Eye* column, Nooks and Crannies of the New Barbarism.) A typical Betjeman note was that the Church Commissioners took it upon themselves to sell off or demolish churches, but accepted no responsibility for their upkeep.

What *Spectator* writers are up to is reinforced by the work of the cartoonists Michael Heath and David Austin. Austin specialises in turning ideas topsy-turvy – a guide-dog turns over the music for a blind pianist. Heath, through the medium of his extraordinarily controlled drawing, is, I think, unrivalled in showing what people look like in any week of any year. And if that isn't funny, I don't know what is.

Christopher Howse

PETER ACKROYD

STARDUST MEMORIES OF WOODY ALLEN

The only person who takes Woody Allen seriously is Woody Allen. 'I've got to find meaning' he announces towards the end of *Stardust Memories*, forgetting that he should have tried much harder to find an audience first. His face has the slackness of an old onion; his hair seems to fall out in clumps whenever he moves; his voice, squeezed with difficulty through those grimly pursed lips, has the whine of a child screaming for more – more of everything. But the eyes betray his age now: sometimes they are tired, with the dazed unknowingness of a man who has stared for too long at his own reflection, and sometimes they're just dead. When he kisses those attractive young actresses – it is Charlotte Rampling here; but as if in self defence, she moves only at half speed – he looks like an old lecher come home to roost. There is something disgusting about a film-maker who lays his fantasies upon an audience with such eagerness and determination. It is also impolite.

None of this would matter if *Stardust Memories* was an interesting film. But it isn't: it is Woody Allen's cinematic memoir, the autobiography of an egomaniac. It is 'written and directed' by him in the way that a mass murder can be said to be both planned and committed. But when actors become self-conscious, they behave very much like reformed whores: too much guilt, and far too much talk. The story here is of a cult figure who has grown tired of his cult; Woody Allen plays a fashionable comic whose adulation has turned him into an object, a possession owned jointly by his film company and his fans. He feels harassed, jaded, out of place, misunderstood: we know this because he tells us so every second minute. It is difficult, however, to sympathise with anyone who takes himself so seriously – and his is not, in any case, an original complaint. Show business exposés of show business account for more hours of boredom in the cinema even than Ingmar Bergman. And when *Stardust Memories* reverts to some of the more outdated tricks of the 'avant-garde' cinema – there is even a film-within-a-film to delight the senior citizens in the audience – the banality of the whole enterprise becomes clear.

Stardust Memories has that knowingness combined with irony that passes amongst cut-price intellectuals as a constituent of a thoroughly modern sensibility. The film has even been made in black-and-white, since this is now the fashionable thing to do. The conventional references are all here – Schopenhauer, suicide, psychiatry, like cheap goods at a white elephant sale held in New York. It is a peculiar feature of Woody Allen's films that he thinks it enough to mention something in order to persuade people that he understands it. In this sense he represents the fine point of American culture, which might be defined as the triumph of vulgarity over barbarism. When he can think of nothing to say, he says it. But he suffers also from another American fault: he assumes that irony is enough. He parodies himself in order to escape external criticism (this is, after all, the theory of modern American art), with a number of jokes and 'one-liners' at his own expense. But he forgets that a fault is actually compounded when it is taken seriously enough to become a joke.

Stardust Memories, then, is a vacuous film. When Woody Allen ceases to be comic, he has nowhere else to go. He seems unable to understand or describe reality, and turns instinctively to the hollow and portentous images of fantasy. He tries to intellectualise without being intelligent, to be witty without first being perceptive. In the process, he is too willing to trust his audience not to get bored – in other words, he expects them to be as interested in himself as he is. Here he has made a fundamental mistake: one tires very quickly of his second-hand insights, his borrowed culture, and his self-conscious naivety. Woody Allen is in love with his own image – and, like some tiny Narcissus, is now drowning in his own inanition.

3 January 1981

WHEN THE VIEWING
HAD TO STOP

There comes a time when Mr Pickwick, bewildered by the horrors of the Fleet Prison, announces that 'I have seen enough . . . My head aches with these scenes, and my heart too. Henceforth I will be a prisoner in my own room.' These are very much the sentiments of your film critic on abandoning his generally undistinguished and no doubt ineffective career; enough is enough. No more films set in what journalists call 'Thatcher's England'; no more tearful tributes to the elderly, starring Katharine Hepburn; no more masterpieces with the subtitles in Americanese. And no more questions from the only mildly curious, on the lines of 'What film is worth seeing?' I never really knew. I never remembered. Yesterday I turned back to the pages of the *Spectator* in 1979, when I began to write film criticism, and I could recall nothing of the films I then either praised or damned. They had gone, vanished, disappeared. I usually find it difficult to recall even the film I saw in the previous week, so effortlessly do the images slip or slide away.

Of course there were some good pictures and, funnily enough, the most memorable are generally the ones which were also the most popular – the films of George Lucas, of Steven Spielberg, of Brian de Palma have lingered in the mind where the work of some of the more apparently 'serious' directors has completely disappeared. Of course there are many cinema critics who, nervous about the status of their chosen field, tend wildly to overpraise any film which has even the remotest chance of seeming 'important': hence the enormous solemnity with which the last film by Tarkovsky was received, when in reality it was nothing more than turgid melodrama. And so it was often with heavy heart that I made my way towards the latest celebrated offering from Eastern Europe, or Japan, or the American 'avant-garde'. There were times when I was agreeably surprised, but there were also times when I was not. In any case I was not a professional or even well-informed film critic. It was always an interest rather than passion, and on Sunday mornings – before writing my review (since Sunday is a day or rest, I always reserve it for journalism) – I would have to scrabble through the newspapers, looking for the names of the director or actors involved in that particular week's offering. As the readers of this journal have probably realised by now, I only ever saw one film a week rather than the statutory three or four; I have to admit, also, that there were times when I walked out of a film before its end. Flesh can only stand so much.

Perhaps more memorable than the films have been the cinemas themselves. There were ghastly places in north London, where health food was sold over the counter; there were dank crypts off the Tottenham Court Road which people used as refuges rather than as places of entertainment. But there were also some agreeable little spots, somehow removed from this world: the Minema is generally billed as the smallest cinema in London but it is also one of the most comfortable, and those who have a taste for macabre interiors should visit one of the auditoria of the Cannon Haymarket. And I regret the passing of the Academy, Oxford Street, which curiously resembled a toy theatre blown up out of all proportion.

And of course the cinema itself was always as important as any of the films being shown in it. The queuing, the buying of undrinkable coffee, the harridans bearing trays of ice-cream, the advertisements for Levi's jeans and the Electricity Board, the warnings about one's handbag, all furnished the slow and cosy passage into the filmic world. And yet even as I enjoyed these simple pleasures I was aware of the fact that they were essentially of an old-fashioned and even anachronistic sort – not ones, perhaps, which will survive the end of the century in their present form. I seemed to be participating in a social activity that was already past; I was still part of the audience that first went to the silent cinema in the Twenties and I was certainly not part of that unimaginable future populace to whom the cinema will mean no more than the penny gaff or the diorama do to us.

So perhaps I am not the right person to answer the usual boring questions. If asked to summarise the state of the British film industry over the last eight years, for example, I would be hard pressed to do so. Certainly I have not noticed any particular improvement in British productions, despite their much heralded 'rebirth', and in fact films which were generally praised – films such as *The Mission* or *Chariots of Fire* – struck me at the time as being more than usually repellent. In a similar way contemporary English film actors seem to have been ludicrously over-praised – ranging from the ubiquitous Bob Hoskins to the even more ubiquitous Jeremy Irons. I suspect that they were in large part lionised because they handily represent, for Hollywood consumption, certain English stereotypes. For what it's worth, after my long spell in front of the silver screen, I would suggest that the two greatest film actors in the world (including men and women) are Robert de Niro and Gerard Depardieu.

When the British film industry is not in question, the argument generally turns on the nature of censorship. There is no doubt that prolonged attendance in the cinema can blunt the sensibility (I am living evidence of this fact), but this is only because film is necessarily a narrow and limited medium which must generally purport to represent 'reality'. Hence the confusion in certain minds, when they mistake film for life. On the other hand, I would not dream of censoring cinematic material, and this because it is equally difficult to know where to start and where to stop. Of course there are rapists or murderers who will blame the latest Channel 4 co-production for their crimes, just as in the last century criminals used to blame their reading of the novels of Harrison Ainsworth, but such death-bed confessions should not be taken too seriously. And, if they are, the consequences might be unfortunate – there was the recent case of the murderer who ascribed his behaviour to an inordinate admiration for the screen persona of Clint Eastwood. Should his films, therefore, be banned? I would be quite happy never to see him on the screen again, but not for those reasons.

I used to be more appalled by violence than by sex; the latter was never particularly interesting, while there were times when the former did genuinely leave me feeling diminished in spirit as well as in imagination. I am also a rather squeamish little person and, despite many years of effort, I found it impossible to sit unbowed through the latest 'horror' epic; I suspect that at least ten per cent of my time in the auditorium was spent with one hand across my eyes – although this was often at the sight of Meryl Streep or Rupert Everett, rather than any more ostensible horror.

So I shall miss nothing in particular after leaving this column – nothing, that is, except an association with the *Spectator* which has remained unbroken since 1973. And what am I most proud of having achieved in these eight years? I am proud never to have used the word 'movie', and of never having had a quotation from one of my reviews used to adorn a cinema advertisement. Goodbye.

7 March 1987

I'm Erik the well-read.

KINGSLEY AMIS

SOD THE PUBLIC:
A CONSUMER'S GUIDE

ABOUT this A–Z: 'Sod the public' is the working slogan not only of government, service industry and retail trade, but also, as 'sod the customer', 'sod the audience' and other variants, that of interior designers, providers of culture, playwrights, composers and many more. For further explanation see CAUSES.

ARCHITECTURE: Most artists, or people who think of themselves as such, have to get the public to watch or listen before they can sod it. The famous pile of bricks at the Tate Gallery was powerless against those who never went to see it, and while still on the shelf *Finnegans Wake* is impotent. Architects are different. They have the unique power of sodding the consumer at a distance, not just if he lives or works in the building concerned, or just when he passes it a couple of times a day, but also when he happens to catch sight of it miles away on the skyline.

ARTS COUNCIL: Grants and bursaries from this detestable and destructive body in effect pay producers, painters, writers and such *in advance.* This is a straight invitation to them to sod the public, whose ticket-money they are no longer obliged to attract, and to seek the more immediate approval of their colleagues and friends instead (see CLUB). The system encourages a habit of thought whereby 'creative' people can be divided into *artists*, who deliver serious, important, innovative, difficult stuff and so of course have to have financial help, and *entertainers*, whose work is easy to understand, enjoyable and therefore popular – you know, like rock music and John Betjeman's poetry, and whose very title to the label 'creative' is shaky. Thus an organisation created to foster art and bring it to the public turns out to be damaging to art and cutting it off from the public. Only those in the trade profit. Compare NATION-ALISED INDUSTRIES and MODERNISM.

CAMRA: The Campaign for Real Ale is an inspiriting but lonely example of rolling back a powerful sod-the-customer tendency. Likely to remain lonely because not all such causes have this one's appeal. Movement for Cleaner Trains? Alliance for Sensible Poetry? It seems unlikely.

CAUSES: The causes, that is, of the phenomena listed. Among them must be centralisation and the tendency to monopoly, the growing power of bureaucrats and experts, and that affluence which has transformed the old relationship between shopkeeper and customer. The shopkeeper need no longer study the customer because if he loses one there will be another along in a minute, and the customer needn't study the shopkeeper because if one purchase goes wrong there is enough money left to try again elsewhere. The question of causes may well be worth following up and a single, primal one may perhaps be discoverable. What has interested me more here has been the diversity and yet the similarity of the effects.

CLUB, how it will go down at the: Where, 100 years ago, a composer or a playwright or a poet was influenced to some degree by what the general public might think of his new work, today such a person is more likely to wonder instead how it will go down at the club, i.e. in the circle of his colleagues, his friends in the profession, certain critics and a more or less specialised and expert section of the public. The effect of this is to drive him towards the technically stimulating, the obscure and the 'sophisticated' and away from the older goals and values of whatever can be called pleasing, straightforward, entertaining, popular; sod the audience, in fact. Over-concern with club opinion is often obvious in modern ARCHITECTURE, in interior design (see PUBS), and in several features of film and television style: thrillers made baffling rather than legitimately puzzling, distracting use of camera, 'clever' cutting and the whole flood of mischievous send-ups, delightful romps, tongue-in-cheek spoofs and hilarious take-offs, particularly to be found in espionage and gangster stories. Nobody outside the industry likes send-ups, as far as I know, though individual examples may be tolerated for their moments of straight action. But a few flip jokes will protect you from being asked by someone at the club, 'Going for teenage market now, Cy?' It may be significant that the outrageous-romp school of spy-crime story has never caught on in printed fiction. See also FILM DIRECTORS and SPECTACLE-FRAMES.

Note: The club in the present sense may well be typified by an actual association or place and its members or habitués, like the Green Room, the BBC Club in Portland Place, the bar at Pinewood Studios and innumerable arty places of resort.

COINAGE, decimalisation of: Never accepted by the public, in that nobody talks of tuppence or fivepence or tenpence, as whoever wished it on us might have thought we would one day, if he thought about it at all – always two p and five p and ten p.

CONCORDE: The turned-down nose of this aircraft is rather ugly. The original straight version looked much nicer, very pretty in fact, but it was discovered that the pilot couldn't see downwards properly from it. Sodding the public does sometimes stop short of actually killing it.

COUNTIES: Changing the names and boundaries of half the counties in Great Britain and abolishing others is an effective way of sodding the citizenry not only on a large scale but for a long time, until all those who remember the old ones are dead, in fact. Except for those who are part of the new system, none of them has ever accepted the change.

DENTISTRY: Once you sat in a chair, now you lie down on a sort of couch. Nastier for you, producing feelings of helplessness among the old and nervous, but nicer for him because he can sit down. A good textbook example of sod the patient.

EFTA: Easier-For-Them Association. Other bodies are obviously at work, like NBC (Nasty But Cheaper) and NKVD (Nanny Knows Very Definitely), but in this country, where the ruling passion is not for more money or power but for less work, EFTA rules.

FILM DIRECTORS: For some reason these have become peculiarly devoted to sodding the customer. Successful ones seem to become so powerful, through their ability to attract star actors and so on, that they can be as self-indulgent, whimsical, mannered and digressive as they please. If a new film comes along and you recognise its director's name, think twice about going.

GPO: So called here to suit my convenience for once in my dealings with it. No need to go over Sunday collection, directories, telephone-boxes, telegrams. One possibly new point: have you ever tried to find out the telephone number of your neighbourhood – or any other – post office? If you knew it, you see, you could ring up and ask about second-class postage to Zaire instead of having to go and queue up to ask.

HOTELS (British): No other institutions quite touch these in their single-minded devotion to the interests of those who work in them and indifference to those of the idiots who use them. Illustrations unnecessary. Motto: 'Can I help you, sir/madam?' i.e. 'What the hell do you want?' Founder-member of EFTA.

JAZZ: The first performers of 'modern' jazz in 1941 showed a remarkably clear sense of what they were doing by *literally* turning their backs on the audience. The first jazz musicians to be given an Arts Council grant were the North-Eastern Jazz Band in 1968.

LAVATORY BOWLS: The old design with a steep inside enabled a reasonably careful gentleman to urinate without spilling a drop. The new (newish) one makes it almost impossible not to bounce a couple on to the floor. But it is *new*.

LIGHT-SWITCHES: When carrying a tray etc. you used to be able to put the light on with your wrist or elbow (and also sometimes open the door-catch in the same sort of way), but now you have to put the tray etc. on the ground or somewhere. Compare TAPS.

MAGAZINES: The growing practice of not numbering advertisement pages, and so forcing the reader to turn through them while looking for what he wants, supposedly makes him more likely to buy and demonstrably sods him at the same time.

MEDICINE: Signs here of a turn of the tide. In America a revolutionary new technique is being developed of asking the patient how he feels on the new treatment, etc, and paying attention to what he says.

MODERNISM: This is an immense subject. For now, consider only that the movement in its very beginnings 80 or more years ago *set out* to 'liberate' the 'artist' (the inverted commas are a bit cheap but are also time-saving) from the need to please or be comprehensible to or otherwise concern himself with the public. 'I believe that a real composer writes for no other purpose than to please himself. Those who compose because they want to please others and have audiences in mind are not artists' – Arnold Schoenberg, who does not go on to say whether or not he considers Mozart, Beethoven and others to be real artists. The undoubted fact that Picasso (and not he alone) was immensely successful says a great deal about the art trade and not much about public taste, except its suggestibility. No modernist composer, film-maker, playwright, poet or novelist has ever appealed to more than a small, specialist group, nor ever will. In this country the movement would probably have expired altogether by now without the life-support machine provided by the ARTS COUNCIL.

MUSIC ON RADIO: There are several musical publics, including a large occasional one (A) that owns and plays some classical records, goes to a concert or the opera a couple of times a year and often listens to music on the BBC when it fancies the selection: and a much smaller one (B) that reads scores, goes to concerts and recitals at least once a week and keeps up with musical developments. What (A) likes best is the period roughly 1770–1920, especially its orchestral and operatic music. Although (B) cannot be described as caring exclusively for 20th-century music, not many in (A) like it much, except for a few special works, chiefly operas. A quick survey shows that the music broadcast on Radio 3 divides about equally between (A) and (B), which considering the respective size of each is sodding most of the public most of the time. (By a terrific concession, about a fifth of the (A) stuff goes out at 7–9 a.m., when the car radios are on.) The point is that (B) is much more influential than (A) – it writes in all the time, it throngs the CLUB – and the programme planners and their staffs inevitably belong to (B). Why should they bother about (A)?

NATIONALISED INDUSTRIES: A recipe for sodding the public by providing an employer who can be struck against indefinitely with no risk of bankrupting him. What was conceived of as the means to general prosperity has notoriously become its chief obstacle. Remember that stuff about production for use and not for profit?

NEW BIBLE AND PRAYERBOOK: A big one, sodding congregation, Church and people at a single stroke. Nobody except those in the trade wanted it.

PACKETS, POSTAL and PACKAGED GOODS: Once, you could open these with your bare hands. Who would think of tackling one today with anything less than a power-saw? But *putting on* the packaging is lovely and quick. Note how on the book-packs they have done away with that little tab-and-tear arrangement down the side, a tiny saving for them and much more trouble for you.

POLITICS: All politicians are, though in varying degrees, sodders of the citizenry, giving them not what they want but what it is felt they ought to have. A British society in which the majority were given what they want would not be attractive to anyone opposed to hanging and flogging, for a start. It should be remembered, however, that if years ago the majority had been given what they wanted about coloured immigration, or not given what they didn't want, a large existing problem would never have arisen.

PUBS: Any pub redesigned internally in the last ten years or so is likely to be uninhabitable (I leave out the question of music, which is a case of the staff sodding the customers.) The designer will usually have concerned himself very little with what the customers might have liked. With what, then? With trend, I suppose, with the ultimate aim of winning a prize awarded by other designers (see CLUB), or having a photograph of the result published in a Swedish magazine. The customers have no way of getting back at the designer and if they go elsewhere they are unlikely to do better. Sodding the public works best either when you are a monopoly (see GPO) or when all or enough of your competitors are sodding it too, a general point perhaps worthy of a heading to itself.

RADIO TIMES: Nobody is going to stop taking this journal because of disgust at its non-programmatic content, and it exploits this strength by sodding the reader in depth. The main departments of this are:
1) Its fairly recently revised and disimproved layout, which makes it even harder than before to find the day and time and service (TV or radio) and channel or frequency (BBC1 or 2, Radio 1, 2, 3, or 4) you are after. In case you are lucky to start with, page numbers are left out where possible (see MAGAZINES).
2) Filling the programme pages with unwanted and often seriously repulsive drawings and interspersing equally unwanted articles in space partly won from.
3) Short-changing you on programme details, especially in casts of films and plays. Even when all the wanted names are there that of one or another character may not be given in full, so that Bill Jones will be just Bill or Jones on the page, not much good when he mostly gets called Jones or Bill on the screen. Radio 3 entries are often minimal, with individual works left untimed in gramophone concerts of two hours or more. (This item, and others on the list, may come rather near grumbling. Perhaps they *are* grumbling, but I would not much care to be the kind of boss who has to go round telling the folks that there are worse troubles at sea.)
All in all *Radio Times* demonstrates most plainly and usefully that those in a position to sod reader, customer and the rest will do so to the limit of their power. (See this list *passim*).

SPECTACLE-FRAMES: All the pairs of glasses I have had for the last 20 years have slipped down my nose within a minute of my putting them on. There is nothing to hold them up, since I lack a convenient trench between my eyes and the side-pieces would not hook round any human ear. The frames are supposed to stay up by gripping the side of my head just above the ears. This doesn't help them to stay up but it certainly hurts my head in those two places. But I bet they looked good photographed in *The Optician*, or whatever that is in Swedish.

SPELLING REFORM: No, not here yet but probably nearer than you think because it has everything required of a quarry for bureaucratic interference, viz:
1) The present system is long established and works perfectly well.
2) No rational person who has given five minutes' thought to the matter wants a change.
3) It would be very expensive. (Transliterating all previous writings for a start.)
4) Any news system would be much worse than the present one. (In this case anything more than tinkering with words like *centre* and *favour* would be unworkable. An alphabet equally intelligible to an Aberdonian, a Chicagoan and a Hararean cannot be devised until we all speak English in exactly the same way. That is probably a little further off.)
5) The most irresistible attraction of the lot to the bureaucrat with a roving eye: the present system is full of illogicalities, inconsistencies, exceptions and things you just have to know, all crying out to be straightened and made uniform.

STAPLES: As paper-fasteners these are more trouble for the recipient than paper-clips but easier for the sender. As ticket-fasteners on dry-cleaned garments they are much more trouble than safety-pins at the receiving end and not that much easier for the people at the shop, but enough to make them worth while.

SUPERMARKETS: A stunning example of a sod-the-customer institution passed off as a public benefit.

TAPS, kitchen and bathroom: If you had oily etc hands you used to be able to turn on the water with your wrist or elbow, now you have to get the oil etc all over the tap before you start. Compare LIGHT-SWITCHES.

THIS YEAR'S MODEL: I think I understand that manufacturers (in the broad as well as narrow sense) want customers to buy anew and that this year's model must look a bit different from last year's to encourage them, and also that customers like to have the latest. I plead only that this year's model should be no more lethal/revolting/inconvenient/uncomfortable/time-wasting/fast-eroding/unnecessarily expensive than last year's.

TRADE UNIONISM: By definition a sod-the-public enterprise, today and for many years. This is now so much taken for granted on all sides that it was scarcely mentioned during the miners' strike.

TYPOGRAPHY: If the newspaper is full of literals, transposed lines, etc, what of it? The reader can sort it out, and if he can't, sod him. Similarly with splitting the line halfway through syllables or in the middle of digraphs. Why not print *chang/ed* or *chan/ged* or *cha/nged*, or *ende/avour* or *que/ue*, or *penk/nife* or *hig/hlight*? Such choppings used to be thought of as discourtesies to the reader, that's to say they're perfectly all right now. Telling the computer it mustn't do things like that takes time.

WEIGHTS AND MEASURES, decimalisation of: Nobody ever wanted this, except bureaucrats and – exporters? Importers? Outside such contexts, adoption of it is a service-able pointer to trendy pissers, as when a broadcaster says a mountain is so many metres high, or someone gives a distance in kilometres (pronounced, of course, kilómetres). Even children taught only the metric system know what feet and miles are.

STOP PRESS: I have just had my new (October 1985) A–D London telephone directory dropped on my doorstep. The outside is newly designed, so that, for instance, the letters A–D on the spine, visible across the room in the 1984 edition, are smaller, pale, sort of italic, because their purpose is not to be legible but to look pretty. Of course.

19 October 1985

'It's funny, really, they call me the waiter, but you've been waiting nearly an hour!'

SOD THE PUBLIC II

ABOUT THIS GUIDE: Introducing my 1985 catalogue (*The Spectator*, 19 October 1985), I wrote: ' "Sod the Public" is the working slogan not only of government, service industry and retail trade, but also, as "sod the customer", "sod the audience" and other variants, that of interior designers, providers of culture, playwrights, composers and many more.' Here are a few supplementary grouches along the same lines with one or two references back to the original.

ACTORS: Actors and actresses are so stupid, ignorant and eaten up with themselves that one can easily forget how lazy they are. Many cannot face the effort of articulating clearly enough to be understood. Of those who can, none bother to speak their lines properly, so as to make sense. In order to do so they would have had to read them through with some care and work out what they meant, asking for help if necessary. They would also have had to discover the general drift of the action and listen to what the other characters might be saying. Anything like that is too much trouble, beside the point, in fact, if all you care about is receiving attention and looking good. So, playing Isabella in *Measure for Measure*, feel absolutely free to say:

> O, it is excellent
> To have a giant's strength, but it is tyrannous
> To use it like a *giant*.

Why not, if that was how you first happened to think of it? And, when another character in another play tells you the bad men are out to kill some third party, nothing of the least importance is to discourage you from saying: 'That's not what *they* want; he's no use to them dead,' – certainly not the reflection that it would make better sense to stress almost any other of the first five words. And, on being told that a situation or event 'was like *that*', go right ahead and say: 'It wasn't *like* that!' instead of 'it *wasn't* like that' because you think you look very strong saying it your way and nobody you care about is actually listening to the words – the bleeding *words*? – least of all the director, who himself only wants it to look right, and is an artist too.

The public has nowhere else to go, except away, and is steadily being reduced to a state in which it listens only in a vague, general and inattentive spirit to the plays, films etc it pays to see. Well, who does it think it is?

ADVERTISING ON TELEVISION: As many had long thought and a recent survey confirmed, the 'good' commercials made by the 'good' directors are hopeless at selling the product. The public is presumably content with the arrangement, though now and again it might prefer to keep the extra couple of coppers on the price and do without the commercial. The customer, in the shape of the vendor or client, has a prima facie case for objection, but these days perhaps the honour and glory (among one's fellows) of having a 'good' commercial attached to one's name outweigh the failure to sell any more actual toffees or insurance. Such must have been the feeling of those who credited the Labour Party with the 'best' television campaign in the 1987 election, and never mind the tiresome and irrelevant fact that the main competing product was favoured instead. The people who counted, those in that sort of journalism and the communications trade, admired it. This time, however, the client might have felt a bit dissatisfied with the deal. I got a frisson when I happened to come across a piece I wrote for the *New York Times* in 1972 about the Nixon-McGovern election campaign. According to the British media, I wrote, the Democratic convention was a spontaneous festival of sweetness and light, the Republican a carefully staged performance rehearsed down to the last hand-clap. In particular, the McGovern campaign film was called 'brilliant', 'beautifully made', projecting him as 'a man of honesty, integrity, physical courage and prescience' [*!!!*]

... 'After rolling around in this warm bath of impending utopian fulfilment,' I continued, 'the fellow who has taken it all seriously gets a sudden dousing of ice-cold water in the form of a tiny paragraph saying that Nixon's lead is up to 29%, down to as little as 24%. What does it mean, such wild divergence between radical opinion and conservative fact? British experience suggests an answer: most people like facts and are conservative, the radical few have the opinions, and the two interests are irreconcilably opposed.'

But perhaps that perception leads us to other pastures than this *Guide*.

ARTS COUNCIL: The days of what in 1985 I rather tamely called 'this detestable and destructive body' are perhaps numbered. Its new chairman, Peter Palumbo, allegedly collects the works of Andy Warhol and is known to have campaigned long, but thank heaven without success, to have an office block in the City of London built by the wrecker Mies van der Rohe.

More to our purpose, he is reported to favour experimental art, which for one in his position comes down to injecting public money into what would otherwise be dead of rightful neglect. Well, one more like him and something may snap somewhere.

BOOKSHOPS: Following a technique pioneered by Foyle's a good 20 years ago, the more 'popular', i.e. lazy and shoddy, bookshops have taken to grouping their (paperback) wares by the publisher, so that unless you happen to know in advance that the works of Anthea Scheissenschreiber are published by Cockroach Books you may have to look round the whole shop before you find them, if indeed they are in stock. Foyle's had wall-lists showing author against publisher, but no doubt it was discovered that the only people benefiting from this arrangement were the public, and it has not been imitated elsewhere. A good example of the workings of EFTA (which see).

BUFFET CARS: These used to stay open until the train had finished its journey; now they shut in time for the staff to tidy up in slow tempo (and block the corridor with their rubbish) and hit the platform at Paddington or Penzance a couple of strides ahead of you and me. So for instance the 15.53 out of Cardiff the other day shut its buffet at 16.05 before terminating at Swansea at 16.46. Having lunched well at Gibson's in Cardiff I was all right, but any poor dabs who got on down the line at Bridgend, Port Talbot Parkway [where?] or Neath had had it. Not a huge atrocity but worth a mention as showing how little bits of sodding the public will burgeon of their own accord in the rich soil of organisations like BR that sod it on the grand scale. Compare the inventive, resourceful skiving of individual postmen, gas or electricity officials and indeed any other public employees.

CLUB, how it will go down at the: Just a reminder of the central truth about contemporary art from poetry to ballet and design from spectacle-frames to pub interiors: the person(s) responsible will show far less interest in the reaction of audience/consumer/public than in that of colleagues/critics/ experts. The exhibition of sculpture may arouse unanimous and heartfelt boredom among ordinary visitors to the gallery, the first performance of the violin concerto provoke at best incomprehension in the concert-hall, the new office-block excite incredulous hostility among all who have to work in it and any passer-by who may chance to catch sight of it. Never mind; the perpetrator is fully satisfied if it goes down well at the club.

EFTA: Easier-For-Them Association. This must have its cadres in every country in the world, even Japan, but is nowhere as powerful as here, where the ruling passion is not for money or power but for less work. (Not so much, by the way, for shorter hours, because more time at home could mean being expected to help in the house.) A growing affiliate of EFTA I missed last time is CBI (Costlier But Inferior), active in production as well as service.

FILM DIRECTORS: It may be just worth suggesting that the much-acknowledged decline in cinema audiences may have been largely caused by the increase in the power and standing of the director, who wants to show he is an artist and be damned to the rest of us, and the decrease in those of the producer, who used to try to please the public. The chronology certainly fits.

MUSIC IN PUBS, ETC: Nearly all pubs now have a sort of music in them, here and there some variety of real music, much more usually what merely shares certain qualities of real music such as pitch, duration etc. Those who like it or benefit from it are the staff of the place, not the public. The staff of course don't *listen* to it, they just want to have it on, in the way that most smokers don't so much like smoking as feel not quite comfortable when not smoking. As regards the public, no doubt some of them would as soon have it on as not, some can ignore it when it isn't loud and put up with it more or less willingly when it is, some hate it so much that they leave and don't come back: those are the ones who like music, a smallish minority, I suppose, in this country at least. We all know about this, but what do we do about it? Does anybody know the relative sizes of the three sections of the public I have tried to distinguish? Do the brewers really do better out of customers who drink against a background (or foreground) of yelling and drumming? Do they, the brewers, think that people over (say) 40 spend or would spend less money in pubs than those under? Is it actually impossible to get staff unless they can 'have it on' all the time? Why is there no campaign on the lines of the brilliantly successful Camra? A pronounceable acronym is needed. Potiphar (Project Outlawing Tintinnabulation In Pubs, Hotels and Restaurants) has it points, except for being overlong, fanciful and forgettable too now nobody has heard of Potiphar. (Well he comes in Genesis xxxix. In the Bible, you know.) Sip (Silence in Pubs) is better. Promise to think about it.

N.B.: This is only partly an age thing and not really a taste thing at all. Restaurants have taken to giving you Mozart with your moules marinière and Bach with your beef: better than drumming and yelling, sure, but not that much. Trying not to be distracted by what you like wastes nearly as much energy as trying to shut out what you abhor.

NEWSREADERS: Another lazy breed like ACTORS. These are likewise too lazy to read through their material before delivering it and constantly misemphasise it, pause in the wrong place, etc. Thus one of them will say forthrightly: 'This morning a Dutch tanker was shot up in the Gulf and this afternoon an *American* destroyer was attacked,' making the viewer wonder foggily whether it was not a Dutch destroyer that was first mentioned. Or just as likely: 'This morning a Dutch tanker was shot up in the Gulf and this afternoon an American *tanker* was attacked,' this time producing foggy wonderment whether it was not an American something-else that was first mentioned. Such readers might plead lack of time for rehearsal, but they are just as bad at nine or ten p.m. with stuff that was in that morning's papers. This excuse cannot cover reporters known as 'correspondents', who are presumably uttering their own words. They recite their pieces, whatever the subject, in a ghastly wheedling singsong, stressing the last word of every sentence no matter how inappropriately, that seems designed to rob them of overall meaning. The public will be able to glean little more than that there has been a bit of a fuss about the air disaster, shake-up health report, Cabinet crisis they read about earlier. Jolly good, because they consequently miss the little leftist distortions the reporter has smuggled in.

RESTAURANTS: It took a spell as a restaurant reviewer to bring home to me that modernism, now in retreat in the arts, has spread to the kitchen and is advancing there by leaps and bounds. The modernist chef sets out not to please the palate but to 'challenge' it. If a helping of roast beef and Yorkshire pudding can be compared to a Constable landscape and a plain grilled sole to a Handel concerto grosso, he will serve you the equivalent of a Picasso figure with both eyes on the same side of its nose or an atonal chamber work for wind instruments by Schoenberg. The bible-cum-Pseuds'-Corner of modernist cooking is the *Good Food Guide* as it has lately become. Here one can read of three-dimensional seasoning and self-congratulatory mousses and note the praise for boldly inventive, innovative, imaginative menus, sauces, combinations of flavours. Jaded by eating out five or ten times a week, food writers have come to seek novelty above everything else and so to encourage chefs to be 'adventurous', to go in for self-expression, to think of themselves as artists and give the writers the excuse to call *themselves* critics. And the trendies go along, though it beats me how anybody can actually prefer to eat, rather than write or read about, a dose of puff pastry 'wrapped around a noisette of lamb and accompanied by a pungent madeira sauce and a garnish of courgettes stuffed with mangetout' to roast leg of lamb with runner beans and baked potatoes. The public just want a decent meal nicely served in a comfortable restaurant, not an exciting bloody gastronomic experience, and are duly sodded. One might have thought that avant-garde cooking, like avant-garde music, drama, etc would soon start needing the support of the Arts Council, but the British will fork out sums in a restaurant that they would never dream of paying for a seat at the opera. I suppose one should be grateful for any lingering sparks of philistinism.

TELEVISION CRITICS: Unlike other classes of critic, these concern themselves with what has already and irrevocably happened, though without ever showing themselves to be the least bit daunted by that thought. In general television critics avoid those programmes that the public actually watch, though they may occasionally stress snooker or soccer coverage to show how quirky or demotic they are, with England's cricketing performances always good for a passing sneer. They prefer to mention Tuesday documentaries or Wednesday plays with a political message acceptable to them or, if not, with some peg on which a political message of their own can be hung.

Although a step further down in esteem, writers who preview television programmes have more actual power. They do their best to put the public off stuff that might be bad for it, using phrases like 'routine [i.e. non-anti-American] spy thriller' or 'uncritical [i.e. non-hostile] account of police work in Liverpool'. Their use of words like 'enjoyable' and of course 'stimulating' or 'irreverent' should be treated with reserve, but they can be useful in alerting one to the threat of private-eye spoofs, tongue-in-cheek Westerns, black comedies and other shopworn novelties dear to retarded directors.

WRITERS' GUILD: This socialist trade union has evolved something called the Minimum Terms Agreement (MTA), whereby a publisher agrees to pay all his authors a minimum advance and a minimum scale of royalties (plus other guarantees). The Guild is trying to make MTA binding on all publishers and so protect all authors from 'exploitation'. If MTA were to be made universal, it would actually create unemployment among authors. There is one highly reputable firm well known for scooping up writers who have failed to achieve publication elsewhere and getting them into print – on terms below the minimum set by MTA. Most budding authors will more or less cheerfully accept such an arrangement (I did myself at that stage). If compelled to implement MTA, the company I refer to would go out of business and a number of writers would be prevented from reaching the public. Like most trade-union deals, this one benefits those in work at the expense of those who are not, and like most interferences with the free market it ultimately disadvantages the very people it was supposedly designed to help.

15 October 1988

TIMOTHY GARTON ASH

WHO NEEDS JOKES?

What is the difference between communists and Christians? Christians believe in life after death; communists in posthumous rehabilitation.

Between socialism and capitalism? In capitalism you have the exploitation of man by man; in socialism it is the other way round.

Between a democracy and a People's Democracy? One is only a jacket; the other a strait-jacket.

And so on. Everyone knows that Eastern Europe is a hotbed of political jokes, a genre quite unlike our own political anecdotes and the delight of visiting academics. 'I was glad to see the jokes are back in force,' comments a professor recently returned from Poland. But the incidence of political jokes is a symptom of a sick polity – an index of unfreedom. In Poland the consumption of political jokes, like the consumption of alcohol, sank dramatically in the Solidarity period: men had better outlets for their political energy and frustrations. It soared with the imposition of martial law. Nazi Germany produced a whole anthology of acid political gibes. East Germany has a regular supply. (In many, only the names have changed.) West Germany has none.

You might think that most jokes originate with so-called 'dissidents' or active opponents of the régime. In my experience this is not the case. The jokesmiths seem most often to be Schweyks, laughing at all serious political engagement, or people who themselves collaborate with the régime in their working hours. The journalist on a party newspaper, the diplomat, the university professor, even the party official, seeks to salvage his self-respect by telling critical jokes in private. They are often a substitute for more serious forms of opposition.

Of course dictators have always feared ridicule, and the most extreme totalitarian dictatorships have punished joke-tellers with death. But in Poland today it is said (jokingly) that the Central Committee has a secret department devoted to the invention of jokes. For the régime they have at least two useful functions. A minor one is that they can be retailed to selected foreign visitors. (Q. What is a 'liberal' communist? A. One who confidentially tells mildly self-critical jokes to his foreign guests.) A major one is that they act as invaluable safety valves for pent-up popular frustrations. They let off steam. In *The Lawless Roads* Graham Greene describes a similar phenomenon in Mexico in the 1930s. 'Always in totalitarian states you get these underground jokes,' Greene comments, 'a bitter powerless humour.'

Powerless! In the short term Greene is surely right. After all, even in a democracy the most brilliant and sustained public satire is rarely seen to change the course of events. At most it may deflate a few overblown individuals, sink the odd cant phrase, expose an unjust act. Witness *Private Eye*. How much less can it change the course of dictatorship! Karl Kraus, probably the greatest satirist of our century, responded to the Nazi rise to power with the words: 'On the subject of Hitler, nothing occurs to me' (*zu Hitler fällt mir nichts ein*). Hitler was not only indescribable, he was beyond the reach of satire. 'Clichés strut around on two legs,' said Kraus, 'while men have their own shot off.' And private quipping, what the Germans call whisperwit (*Flüsterwitz*), is much less of a threat than public satire. Psychologically, it can be an *aid* to public conformity.

So the jokes pour like rain off the stone ramparts of power. The rain looks 'powerless' but in the end it is the rain which wears down the stone. The constant acid drizzle of political humour in Eastern Europe has surely contributed to the long-term erosion of the régimes' credibility. Future historians should turn to collections of these jokes for a brilliant survey of popular discontents, a comprehensive indictment of the existing socialist system – an index of unfreedom. Here they will find the pithiest commentaries on the ubiquitous shortages, the lies and evasions of propaganda, the censorship and the restrictions on freedom of movement, the privileges and inequality, the pull of the West:

What is a string quartet? An East German orchestra after a tour in the West.

Why do the butchers always leave one sausage in the window? So that people will not start queuing for tiles.

You know what happened when they introduced socialism to the Sahara? Within a year there was a shortage of sand.

I have heard versions of this last joke for almost every country in the world. An especially rich source will be the imaginary listeners' questions and régime answers on the fictional 'Radio Jerewan'. A listener asks: 'How many weeks' wages does an American worker need to buy a car, and how quickly can he obtain it?' After a long silence the state radio replies: 'But they kill negroes.'

I have no doubt that there are already acid jokes about Korean airliners and Soviet responses. ('But the Americans have spies.')

Did you hear that they have released Agca? The KGB has proved that the Pope drew first.

As Greene suggests, you will find these 'underground jokes' in all totalitarian states. But there are several reasons why they are particularly sharp and abundant in Eastern Europe. All ideologies which claim to have an answer to every question, a final solution to all problems, are ultimately ridiculous, but Marxist-Leninist ideology is particularly ill equipped to explain what is happening in Eastern Europe today. When ideologists are reduced to saying that a spade is 'objectively' a pickaxe, the jokesmiths have an easy time. Humour always explores the gulf between ideology and reality, preaching and practice, and nowhere is this gulf wider. Witness the joke about Poland's communist leaders who, in despair, hold a seance to consult the ghost of Lenin. Lenin's answer to their problems: 'Arm the workers!'

Another reason for the special quality of East European political jokes is that they are the direct successors to, and benefactors of, the most brilliant humour of the oppressed which the world has ever recorded: the Jewish/Yiddish humour of the European centuries before Hitler. Indeed, some of them still preserve the Jewish forms:

Rabbi, can one build socialism in one country? Yes, my son, but one must live in another.

The phone's dead.

Rabbi, will there be a Third World War? No, my son, but one day the 'Struggle for Peace' will become so fierce that no house will be left standing.

Of course, until recently this area was also a breeding-ground for the worst anti-semitic gibes. But I must say that I have heard more anti-semitic jokes in Britain and America than I have in Poland. This is no doubt partly because there are only a few thousand Jews left in Poland. Instead, recent years have seen grotesque attempts by one faction in the Polish Communist Party to whip up anti-semitism without Jews. These attempts gave rise to the blackest joke which I have ever heard, or hope to hear. It was told in Poland in 1981.

Do you know why there is a shortage of soap? Because the authorities are trying to turn the soap back into Jews.

This is the authentic note of the humour of the oppressed, as black and bitter as the reality it describes. This would not be retailed by 'liberal' communists to their foreign guests. We return home with the wine, and forget the trampling of grapes which made it.

In Brecht's *Galileo* the great scientist is reproached bitterly after his recantation with the words, 'Unhappy the land that has no heroes.' 'No,' Galileo replies. 'Unhappy the land that has need of heroes.'

When I think of the trampling of human beings which goes into the making of those vintage jokes I say, 'Unhappy the land that has need of jokes.'

17 September 1983

JEFFREY BERNARD

MAURICE

As Maurice Richardson would have appreciated, it's bad enough having to write at all, but to have to write about him in the past tense is a horribly sad business. God only knows how the writers of obituaries go about their craft. I certainly couldn't write one; but the man deserves more than a mention and for some odd reason I couldn't find one in either The *Times* or the *Sunday Times*. Perhaps I simply missed a mention but, in any case, and to use the obituary writer's cliché, Maurice is certainly going to be sadly missed. He was a remarkable bloke.

He struck me as being a pretty classic example of a manic-depressive, but I should have checked up with him on the matter, since it wasn't just one of his pet subjects but one that he was an expert on. Psychology apart Maurice knew loads about snakes, Gene Tunney, what fools we are, the inhabitants of Fleet Street and Soho and he knew slightly less than he would have have liked to about horse racing.

I remember him best when I lived in Suffolk about six miles down the road from him. We'd both be driven by sheer boredom to a pub in Sudbury every Thursday, which was market day and, the boredom of country life apart, we met there because the pub was open all day on market days. We did quite a bit of chuckling together about the extraordinary landlord on the premises. He was new to the game and he used to charge us only 20p for Pernod and Ricard and so Maurice and I drank large ones. One day the landlord asked Maurice, 'I'm not sure I've got it right. Don't you think I ought to charge more for the stuff?' Maurice winked at me and, turning to our host, he said, 'Oh no. My dear chap this is simply rubbish from France. It makes people go blind in Marseilles. Gentlemen simply don't touch it. No, no. Twenty pence is just right.'

I mentioned Maurice being something of a manic-depressive because it strikes me now that I only met Maurice in his manic moments. On other occasions I assume he was at home or at home and working. Anyway, these manic moments were at once funny and embarrassing. His voice used to positively boom out and on the train we used between Sudbury and Liverpool Street I have to admit that on occasions I pretended I wasn't with him. Typical of Maurice was the time when we were standing in the buffet car surrounded by solicitors, City gents and what have you – all of them pin-striped and serious. Maurice was getting them in as they say and he turned round to me and, shouting over everyone's heads, he said, 'D'you know what I think I'll do this evening? I think I'll go to Ipswich and have a whore.' It was said with a terribly superior voice and I have his permission to tell you since he once said that when a man was dead that was just when you should say anything about him.

He was impeccable in his folly though. His betting slips were immaculately written out – something he'd roar with laughter about – and his occasional offers of violence were most gentlemanly, as though he were proposing a duel in the grand old manner. He didn't suffer fools gladly and I remember him summing them up very briefly and with great disdain saying, 'Oh him. He's a frightful little shit.' Conversely, of an ex-boxer down on his luck or someone he liked who'd gone bust in the betting shop. 'Oh yes. Nice chap. Needs to be bought a drink. What?'

When I was down on my own luck and drying out for two-and-half years Maurice was never off the telephone to me or my nurse. He took a sudden interest in alcoholism and he suddenly regretted the fact that Freud had had so little to say about it. Of course, he had to have his joke. 'Still on the wagon?' 'Yes, Maurice,' I'd reply. He'd then roar with laughter, say, 'Well done,' and add, quite unnecessarily, 'I'm not.' Further peals of laughter and collapse of elderly party.

Finally, I remember meeting Maurice for the first time. It was in the old Mandrake Club. 'What are you going to do?' he asked me. 'I'd like to write,' I said. 'Oh, I shouldn't do that,' he said, 'It's a frightful business. Have a drink instead.' Thank you, Maurice.

7 October 1978

QUARKERY

In my desperation to get away from journalism I'm seriously thinking of bluffing my way into entirely new fields of work. My bad luck though stems from a very ordinary public school education which equipped me to do precisely nothing. Not one thing that held my interest in the classroom has been of any use to me since, and what I learned between lessons, manners and the foxtrot, is rusty and obsolete. So, I've been scanning the newspaper ads for vacancies and the only jobs I've come across that might possibly enable me to continue to live like an impoverished lord are those that I'll simply have to bluff my way into.

I'm tempted to apply for quite a few academic posts and they're crying out for lecturers in English Literature in the Middle East and darkest Africa. The way I see it, I'll set my students the task of reading something like *Middlemarch* and then ask them to write a 5,000-word essay on it, by which time I'll not only be tumbled and fired but will have been at it long enough to get a diamond handshake. Then, of course, everyone needs doctors in all those outbacks and I reckon, armed with a few text books and tools of the trade, I'd last a good three months – if not as a flying doctor then one with a taxi.

Ideally, I'd like a *Spectator* reader to lend me a modest £10,000 so that I could open a bar restaurant by a West Indian beach; but as that's not to be – you fools – then it's got to be the gem of a job I saw advertised in The *Times* last week. It went like this. 'Postdoctoral Research Fellow. Applications are invited for a post of Postdoctoral Research Fellow to work on the computer-simulations of 10^{14}–10^{16} eV cosmic-ray extensive air showers and to join an SRC-supported research group under the direction of Dr A. L. Hodson using a $42m^3$ array of current-limited spark chambers and a $3m^2$ cloud chamber to investigate sub-cores and high pt phenomena in air showers and to search for e/3 quarks near shower axes.'

Well, that job just has to be a walkover – a complete doddle. I particularly like the idea of searching for the odd quark which is, as we all know, a cross between a duck and a dog and not to be confused with the Dog and Duck in Frith Street. I'm pretty sure that the crucial hours of this laboratory bluff would be those in the first day at work. There'd be numerous introductions – lingering a little over those to my female colleagues – and then I suppose Dr Hodson would let me settle in to my bench or office before chatting me up over the ubiquitous instant coffee. I can hear him now.

'Well, Doctor Bernard, tell me, why did you leave your last post?' 'Funny you should ask that. Yes. Ha, ha. As a matter of fact, and although I say it myself, it was due entirely to professional jealousy.' 'Jealousy? How come?' 'Well, you see, I was finding so many quarks without even going anywhere near the shower axes let alone using an almost zero-rated, current-limited spark chamber that they simply couldn't stand it. Mind you, I was glad to go and I'm glad to be here where, I understand, I'll be able to work largely on my own.' 'Quite.' 'Any more of that coffee before I roll my sleeves up?' 'Yes, of course.' 'That reminds me. Is there anywhere decent to eat lunch around here?' 'Well, we do have a canteen which I'm sure you'll find amply . . .' 'Oh no. I like to get away during the lunch hour. Never could stand shop talk. Devoted as I am to research I wouldn't want to take a quark with me to lunch. Ha, ha.' 'Quite.' 'Right, let's get at those extensive air showers then. Hang on.' 'What is it doctor?' 'I've just noticed the time. It's 10.30 already.' 'Indeed it is.' 'Well, we're in Cambridge aren't we. They open at 10.30 here don't they?' 'They?' 'The pubs, old man. Come on. You know what makes Doctor Jack a dull boy, don't you?' 'Well, er, yes. I suppose I could show you our immediate environs if you wish it.' 'Come on then. Those sub-cores won't run away before closing time, will they?' 'No, I suppose not, but I'm not sure we should be . . .'

For a very few days I might just be considered a mad, eccentric genius before the boot and a month's wages. But that would just about tide me over until I started drilling for oil for BP or lecturing in chemistry at Roedean.

9 August 1980

TALKING POINTS

I was lying in the bath this morning thinking, for no good reason, how much the Pope looks like the man who used to run Bianchi's when the radio announced a weather forecast that reminded me of a typical married day of yesteryear. After a bright start it was going to be cold and dry. The evening would be chilly. Ring any bells to any of you chaps out there? Yes, perhaps God has been trying to give me hints and clues for years. Perhaps they've never really been talking about the weather. They've been talking about the lady of the moment all the time. 'After a frosty start to the day a depression will bring fog and mist to many parts. By late evening visibility will be very poor and the night will be cool.' But, of course, it's only to women that weather means weather, and the old cow downstairs personifies the English obsession with the weather while boring for England at the same time.

'Ooh, it was cold last night Mr B. I said to Bill I said, "Bill, *you* can take the dog out tonight. *I'm* not going out there. Not for anything." Then it came down. Did it come down. I mean did you hear it?' 'No.' 'What, you didn't hear it?' 'No.' 'Ooh, you must sleep well. You do sleep well don't you Mr B?' (She is letting me know she knows I drink.) 'Well you're lucky. It takes one drop of rain, that's all, one drop of rain and I'm wide awake. Mind you I don't mind the rain. I mean rain's all right if you're covered up properly. It can't hurt you, can it? No, it's the wind I can't stand. You can give me all the rain you want but you can keep your wind. Ooh, what *am* I saying. No, when we went away to Margate last year the wind was fierce. We were on the beach and I said to Bill, "Bill, we're going home." Yes, I put my foot down. Still, should be nice today. Sun's trying isn't he?' 'Yes.' 'Off to work then?' 'Yes.' 'I expect you must be very busy.' 'Pretty.' 'I don't know how you do it. I tried it once.' 'Really?' 'Oh yes. I used to jot my thoughts down in a little book. You know, just for fun. But I never showed it to anyone. No, I couldn't do that. They'd think I was silly wouldn't they?' 'No, I'm sure they wouldn't.' (Shut up you hideous, stupid, old cow before I strangle you.) 'Oh yes they would. If I'd had your sort of education, mind you, I might.' (If you'd had my sort of

33

*"You think you've got problems, I've been trying
to drink myself to death for thirty years".*

education you disgusting person – sudden picture in my mind
of disgusting person's bare buttocks being caned – you might be
jotting your thoughts down for the *Guardian*.) 'No, I'm sure
your little book's very interesting. Anyway, look, I must dash.'
'Off to the desk and the typewriter then? I expect you've got a
nice office, haven't you?' (Yes, it's got a 20-foot desk with eight
stools along it and four beer pumps behind it, you ghastly
person.) 'Oh well, I shan't keep you. Look, there it is. I knew
that old sun would pop out. Chilly though, isn't it?' 'Yes.
Right. Be seeing you. Bye.' 'Mind you wrap up then.' (Mind
you wrap up altogether you horrible slug.)

God preserve us. But did he hell. I got to my office half an
hour later, and there was a new barmaid. And what did this
mindless person say to me while idly polishing a glass? 'Never
mind. Each day we get a little nearer to heaven, don't we?'
There's no answer to that. I was rendered speechless. Each day
we get a little nearer to heaven! I ask you. Here's me trying to
avoid heaven like the plague – I wonder what time they open

there, or do they open at all? – and there's this benign tumour over the bar proving that the 'meaning of life' isn't worth contemplating since there isn't one if such people exist. Wouldn't I like to give them all the leg up to heaven straight away, though. But if you can't beat them, join them. 'Christ it's chilly, isn't it?' I said. 'Ever so. I expect that sun'll pop out soon though.' 'Yes,' I said, 'you can't keep a good man down. Ha, ha.' 'Ha ha.' 'Brr, brr.' 'Hands cold?' 'Ooh, yes. Brr.'

28 November 1981

IN A PICKLE

I read that a member of the General Medical Council has called on his colleagues for quicker identification and treatment for alcoholic doctors. The article, in the *Times*, was headed 'Alcoholic Doctor Tells How He Fought Back'. There are two things that interest me here: firstly the business of identifying an alcoholic and secondly the matter of fighting back. How on earth they can have trouble in not identifying an alcoholic immediately, heaven alone knows. I can spot one a mile away. But could they spot my friend Keith I wonder? They must be blind as bats. Anyway, Keith woke up one day sitting in pitch darkness. He groped around for a while and realised slowly that he was in a cinema. Further groping got him to an exit door and he eventually got out on to the street. He didn't know what town he was in but made his way to a pub where, with great embarrassment, he asked the barman where he was. 'Dover,' he was told. Then it all came back to him. 'Christ Almighty,' he said. 'I got married yesterday.' I can put the General Medical Council in touch with several Keiths, but I suppose only the 3,000 out of 81,000 alcoholic doctors in this country would be able to identify them quickly.

But we must help the medical profession and give them some clues. A man I know once went to a literary booze-up and walked over to a glass, fronted bookcase to see what sort of stuff his host had to read. To his amazement there were no books in the case, only John Raymond standing there in a stupor. I myself once woke up in Cowes of all places and I have even woken up in a drawer at the bottom of a wardrobe. That was fairly frightening. Try opening a drawer from the inside. It's quite tricky. Then we have our hero on the *Mirror*. I've mentioned him before but, for the benefit of doctors, he is worth recalling. He broke into a pickle factory one night with his girlfriend with the purpose of laying her and fell into a vat of chutney. Then we have the doctors themselves. There were two of them, patients like myself in 1972 in Max Glatt's ward in St Bernard's Hospital. One of them was addicted to barbiturates. He didn't interest me, no drug addicts do, but I asked the alcoholic doctor how did he first know he was an alcoholic and he told me, 'When I sprayed vaginal deodorant on a man's face.'

But the business of the doctor telling how he 'fought back' gets me. I fought back too. I fought back from two and a half years of the most boring, depressing desolation of sobriety you can imagine. I wouldn't go on the wagon again for all the tea in China. For two and a half years I felt apart from the human race. The day I cracked in 1976 I called round to my friend Eva and we cracked a bottle of scotch. Then we went round to the Dover Castle – always full of doctors – and we met up eventually with Frank Norman and drank more scotch. After all those years a bottle of the stuff is damn nigh a killer. Of course it is poison. Frank took me to the Connaught for breakfast the next day and I thought I was going to die. The fact that I'm here now and that Eva and Frank are dead seems unfair.

To go back to the doctors: they apparently consider heavy drinking to be more than four pints of beer a day. I should have thought that to be the national average lunchtime consumption. But just listen to this. 'I do not remember ever making a mistake, but one of the worst aspects of alcoholism is that you black out. One day I had to ring up the surgery to make sure I had done one of my visits the night before.'

Well, surprise, surprise. What I want to know is, if he blacked out how the hell does he *know* he never ever made a mistake? The wrong leg off? I know I've had the wrong leg *over* because I too have had to ring up the surgery to find out where and if I had done one of my visits the night before. I just don't understand how doctors can be so naive. Well, I do. It's the old business of all that time at school and then in hospital and not seeing anything much of life itself. The Middlesex ought to send their students along to the Coach. They'd find ample opportunity to practise spotting and identifying alcoholics. They're the ones smiling.

27 August 1983

FAVOURITES

It's been a particularly soft and uninteresting week. So I shall have to diversify. Firstly, foremost and most awful, John Le Mesurier died. Then Dave Smith, known to all as 'Chicago' died, and Barclaycard are taking me to court. John Le Mesurier was a really lovely man. He was superficially and slightly like the sergeant he played in *Dad's Army* but deeper down he was simply a kind, good bloke who, unlike many actors, had subjects and objects of conversation more than most actors. Years ago, we spent a wonderful weekend at Dan Farson's house in North Devon. There was John, me and a busty, blonde Australian girl I'd recently discovered with the ghastly name of Darlene, Sandy Fawkes, Tom Hawkyard and an enormous fresh salmon that Dan had seemingly plundered from the beaches. (Dan is and was a great cook.)

It was during that weekend that John and I discovered that we had a mutual liking, loathing, contempt and amusement for clichés. We started collecting them and vowed we'd do a dictionary of clichés. John's favourite was: 'You can't be too careful' (muttered after a trivial complaint by a pub landlord), and mine was always – still is – 'You only get out of life what you put into it'. Of course there were and are others like, 'An idle mind is the playground of the devil'. But John Le Mes had a real and true sense of the absurd which made him a bit exceptional. He was so very good playing the *straight* part of Kim Philby in *The Traitor* and he really could act, 'translate', as Nadia Boulanger might have said. Not all was easy on the eye and ear comedy. He could do it. So there. Another one gone.

In the same week went Dave Smith, a pillar and part of the establishment of the French pub, known to all and sundry as

37

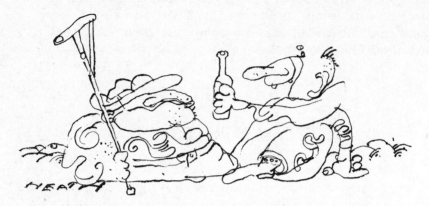

"I think you may find that this makes you
amusingly mindless"

'Chicago'. A pretty good middleweight in his day – the 1920s –
he fought Battling Siki for the championship of the world and
once tangled with Marcel Thil who was champion. In his old
age he became delightfully confused as opposed to punchy. A
few years ago, this great, big, irrepressible spade was in hospital
and gave Gaston Berlemont, the govnor of the French pub, as
his 'next of kin'. Lovely Maurice Richardson wrote a nice piece
about Chicago – in the *Observer* I think – and he too, like John
Le Mesurier will be sadly missed.

It's inevitable, I suppose, that the older you get the more
times you find yourself writing obituaries of sorts. It's a rotten
business. So far I've found it to be 2–1 against women. I'm not
quite sure why they last that little bit longer. Could they be that
little bit more sensible than men? But John Le Mes was 71 and
sensible – although always terribly worried and rather sad – and
should surely have snuffed it before 71. I suppose that the ladies
tend to have two feet on the ground as opposed to one foot in
the grave.

One of the most ghastly stories that amused John so much
was of the incident some 25 years ago when he nearly did snuff
it in a hospital in Gibraltar. That mad, eccentric actor, Dennis
Shaw, phoned him from the Intrepid Fox, a pub in Wardour
Street, making a transfer charge call and saying: 'Hallo, old

man. I hear you're dying.' A shocked John said, 'Am I really? What d'you want?' Dennis just said, 'Send me ten bob, old man.' John Le Mes always liked that tale. It may have been a part of his favourite question when slightly pissed: 'What's to become of us all?' You tell me, John.

26 November 1983

TRICKSTER

After obituaries it's the latest wills column in the *Times* that catches my eye in the mornings. It's not that I'm expecting a legacy but, like the child looking into a sweetshop window, I'm fascinated by the amounts of money I'm never ever going to sink my teeth into. Incidentally, the sums left by seaside resident widows and rural spinsters seem only to be surpassed by East Anglian farmers. Presumably they kill off so many husbands, families and pigs that they can't hope to get through what they've got. But what's got me thinking about wills at the moment is one that I saw last week. It said that a Lancashire chemist by the name of Arthur Skelton had left something in the region of £110,000 and if it was the Arthur Skelton I knew then I want to know where the hell my dividend is.

But it just can't be. We all knew my Arthur Skelton as 'The Pox Doctor's Clerk' and that's how you must have known him if you were bumming around in the Charlotte Street area some 25 years ago. I don't think that Arthur did actually ever render clerical assistance to a genito-urinary specialist but he had one of those unfortunate faces that made you think he might have if you happened ever to think about that sort of thing in the first place. He was refined/shabby which made him look as though he might have pushed a modest pen, but, he was also grubby so that you wondered where on earth he might be doing it, added to which he had the washed-out eyes of a man who was up to here in it. No, he could never have accumulated £110,000 although I know he dabbled in abortion.

Anyway, my Arthur, the Charlotte Street one, was a remarkable man. When he first arrived in the Soho area he'd just been released from prison having served a three-month sentence for an act of gross indecency committed on Blackpool beach on an August Bank Holiday. He was something of a showman in his modest way you see. The trouble though with Arthur was that his sights were always set so terribly low. As a confidence trickster he lacked one vital thing – self-confidence. He couldn't see beyond the next ten shillings because, like a lot of bums, money didn't really suit him. I doubt very much whether he could stand the terrific pressures of life at the bottom today but that's by the by. What I meant to tell you about was the Middlesex Hospital incident which just about summed Arthur up and which makes me sure that the one mentioned in the *Times*'s wills must have been yet another Arthur.

I'm going back a bit now to the days when it was sometimes necessary to work and Arthur was showing willing for a week doing a spot of portering at the Middlesex. Wheeling food trolleys and corpses about, I suppose. Anyway, during the week he worked there he made a number of spectacular if bizarre appointments with people he hoped to extract trivial sums from. For this purpose Arthur 'borrowed' a green surgeon's gown, mask and boots – all the trimmings in fact – and then arranged with his would-be creditors that they should meet him at a side entrance of the hospital.

Faced by the extraordinary Arthur these people would be told, 'Look, can you let me have ten bob immediately? I'm in the middle of performing a very important brain operation and I've only got a moment. I'll pay you back tonight in the Black Horse.' A truly amazing bit of nonsense and one that raises a few interesting points as to the gullibility of some folk and the richness of a man's mad fantasy life.

In the first place I'm fascinated by the word 'important' as applied to a brain operation. Can there possibly be such a thing as a unimportant brain operation? Secondly, does one pause during a brain operation for tea or a smoke, never mind an attempt to borrow money? Thirdly, what manner of brain surgeon needs a paltry ten shillings? It seems that neither the incredible Arthur nor his stupid victims questioned such matters.

Of course, had Arthur moved on to take up residence in some

North Country hospital or even abroad in an American hospital, I suppose he just might have accumulated enough ten bobs to be the Arthur Skelton who left £110,000 according to the *Times*. In that happy event I think that at least I might be mentioned in someone's will. After all, I was very good to Arthur. I bought him cups of tea when he was skint, but I drew the line at allowing him to practise on me.

17 December 1983

BYE BYE BLACKBIRD

It's been another rather silly week in the back garden of Soho. On Monday I met a black bird with thrush and, as I predicted in last week's column, the drama student didn't last long. Lingering over a pot of Earl Grey at the end of an afternoon seminar – included in the service charge – she casually dismissed King Lear as being an old man with woman troubles. I was so irritated I asked her to remove her toothbrush from my bathroom beer mug and make other arrangements for her future unhappiness. Such people come here in taxis but they leave in buses and it serves them right. Well, later that evening –back at the drawing board so to speak – in Kettners and sipping Cointreau, the poor man's pre-frontal lobotomy, these tired old eyes came to rest on this delightful looking black bird who omitted to tell me that she had thrush until I had actually signed her into the Great Portland Street Academy. I've put her on a crash course of natural yoghurt which rather messily has to be applied to the parts as well as swallowed and I've sworn her to celibacy until the start of the flat racing season, which opens at Doncaster on 22 March, exactly one day after J. S. Bach's birthday. You could now call her a bird in the bush and I fear I have none in the hand. The next morning I perked up a bit when the telephone rang and I heard the soft voice of my Dublin bookmaker. He told me that Capture Him, held in the highest esteem by his trainer Vincent O'Brien, must be backed when he comes to England in the spring and possibly for the 2,000 Guineas. But that's by the by and I only mention it since the information comes from the same source that gave us Bajan Sunshine for last year's Cesarewitch.

At lunchtime, Charlie took me to a rather superior fish and chip shop where they gave us some tepid white wine in teacups after hours. They meant well but it was quite disgusting. Wheelers have got it right. If you make it cold enough you can drink Château Filth without noticing it. Anyway, the plonk went to my head and I ordered a suit I can't pay for on my way home. Which reminds me. The Inland Revenue finally got me to court last Friday and they're going to tap my income at source for the next 13 months. I think I slipped up badly. I made the wretched collector an offer which he accepted with such alacrity that I knew immediately I'd gone over the top. Can you imagine writing something like 60 columns for practically nothing? So, if I sound a little churlish here until next year's Grand National you'll know it has nothing to do with thrush or drama students. I managed to needle the collector though. What these people don't like or understand after you've been pleading poverty in the dock is one's hailing a taxi outside the court instead of jumping on a bus. That's why they're tax collectors who'll never know the invigorating joys of treading water in the deep end without a life belt.

But something will turn up and a bit did on Thursday. An extremely shrewd television producer called round in the morning and asked me if I'd like to go on the box and talk about the low life, how I got into it and why I like it. Now, for three minutes that would be something of a doddle but this man says it's for 28 minutes straight into a camera. Twenty-eight bloody minutes! If the film doesn't end up in the cutting room dustbin I want you to watch it – I'll tell you the date when I know it – to see how a person can destroy themselves with their own vanity. It's something I've always wanted to do and it will probably turn out to be as farcical as my courtroom appearances. Every time I go to court I expect to see the famous titter go around the court. I think I'm going to be as witty as Oscar Wilde and have everyone in stitches with the judge spluttering 'Not guilty' at the end of the proceedings. What happens is a bit of grovelling and an inane and insincere apology followed by several stiff drinks in the nearest pub. Not the happy hour, but the remorse hour.

Just before I went into hospital – and this is a sordid story that warrants no detail – I collected a criminal record for kicking someone's car parked annoyingly on the pavement. A CID plain-clothes man arrested me in the Coach on a charge of criminal damage and took me to Vine Street where I was fingerprinted and photographed. But this is extraordinary. As we walked past the Swiss pub on our way to the nick the arresting detective said, 'You screwed the landlord's daughter here in 1976, didn't you?' Well, I was amazed. How anyone could have known what went on that Christmas Day after lunch on the saloon bar floor after the guvnor went upstairs for a nap I'll never know. But I liked the magistrate at Bow Street when I went up for the car kicking. He looked at my record and saw I'd been nicked last October for going over the top in the Raj of India restaurant and said, 'The last time it was rubber plants, Mr Bernard. Now it's cars. What next?' Well, you tell me, I thought. Probably a collector of taxes, possibly a drama student, maybe a black bird with the treble up of thrush, herpes and AIDS. All I know is that when I leave this flat it gets bloody dangerous. No wonder vultures are nesting on the roof of the Coach and Horses.

3 March 1984

"I've enjoyed my life, any failure or unhappiness I've had I been able to blame on my husband".

A FRIEND INDEED

It may be more difficult to make new friends as you get older but it is some consolation to know how easy it is to lose them when you are young. Take George. He was befriended by a terribly nice old lady who upon seeing his socks through the soles of his shoes invited him down to her country estate for a gentle weekend party. It went swimmingly and with some grace until late in the evening and after a splendid dinner when George crashed out on the sofa. They kindly left him there to sleep it off. He awoke in the middle of the night – desperate for a pee – in the pitch-dark room and began to grope his way around in search of the light switch. At one point he stuck his hand into a glass object which was very wet indeed. Still he went on groping until he eventually found his target and when he did get the lights on he beheld to his horror that he had put a hand in an inkwell and that the subsequent groping had covered the walls, including a tapestry, with ink. He surmised, probably quite rightly, that the tapestry might be worth a shilling or two and he fled into the night and drove back to London.

Two weeks later he was strolling along the Kings Road, as silly young men are wont to, and he bumped into his hostess's son. He confessed. The truth poured out. The son told him not to worry so much and that she was really very fond of George. 'Just write her a letter of apology and it'll all be forgotten in no time.' George sat down in his club and did just that. The old lady was very pleased and she wrote back to George asking him to come and have tea in her London house the following week. George arrived at the appointed time and there were crumpets and China tea on the table. All very pretty. She then directed George to a sofa and upon sitting down he felt a strange wriggling under his bottom. His fear of seeming eccentric or difficult again determined him to stay firmly rooted to the spot. Anyway, all was forgiven and they were friends again. Even the wriggling subsided into a warm stillness. When the time came for George to take his leave the old lady got up to summon a maid to show George out. He turned around and saw that he had been sitting on her chihuahua which was now very truly dead. In another blind panic he stuffed the dog in his bag, took his leave, and then put it in the next door neighbour's dustbin. I can't help making conjectures as to George's subsequent career but I like the cut of his jib.

He could possibly be related to the other man I heard about last week as well who was extremely drunk at his own wedding in a church. He'd had so much the night before at one of those ghastly stag parties that he stood in front of the altar swaying. He was then suddenly sick over the bride. No one said a word or moved a muscle save the dear little bridesmaids who solemnly dipped their hankies into a flower vase. (You will note that nothing disturbs the English middle class. They go on through anything as though nothing has happened.) The service continued a while and then the groom was sick again, this time over the vicar. Now all this was seen by the sweet choirboys who, strangely squeamish for little boys and not as used to adult middle-class behaviour as *Spectator* readers, all began to be sick themselves one after the other. Perhaps, and I fear, we shall never know how the couple conducted events on their wedding night. I would like to think that George and the nameless bridegroom share a flat. They could well swap roles but although I have a deep-rooted hatred of chihuahuas I think we should draw the line at being sick over them.

17 August 1985

THE WOOLWICH TRAIN

Soho's leading fantasist, the man who raced his cats years ago when bad weather ruined the National Hunt programme, has plucked another one out of thin air. He told us in the Coach and Horses the other day that he had been having sexual intercourse with a woman who, in the middle of the proceedings, announced that she voted Conservative. It offended his socialist principles so deeply that he threw her out of his bed and into the street. So he tells us. It matters not a jot that he would be so lucky to get *anyone* to bed that he would keep them prisoner there until the food, gas, light and his libido had run out. No, what puzzles us is just how the hell he managed to elicit such information from a lady at such a time as that. Would he in the middle of the thrashing about and his passion be moved to enquire, 'By the way, what do you think of Mrs Thatcher?'? I think it doubtful and I would also think, were I the lady, which heaven and hell forbid, that I had not quite got his undivided attention while the world shook and earth moved.

He thinks these things up on the train, you know. Every morning he travels from Woolwich to Charing Cross and by the time he arrives in the pub something extraordinary has happened to him or he has contrived an extraordinary happening. I think it is very bold of fantasists never to question one's credulity. Either that or he thinks we're all daft as brushes. Take the incident of the 15 Woolwich black men. He claims he saw a man in his local refused a drink by the landlord because he was black. Outraged – and quite rightly so, had the incident taken place – he went out into the street and gathered unto himself 15 black men, marched them into the pub and insisted on buying them a pint of lager each. That'll show the ghastly landlord, he thought.

There are just two points here I think we should look into. Firstly, are there 15 black men in Woolwich and if so why would they all at once be together within strolling distance of the pub? Secondly, 15 pints of lager would have cost approximately £16 and that is one hell of a round for anyone in a Woolwich pub let alone a man with invisible means. And incidentally, isn't it rather long odds against all 15 black men being lager drinkers? Would he have done the same for 15 Chinamen in Greenwich?

But the woman who announced her Tory sympathies while he was making love to her – and I use the phrase 'make love' in case children might read this, he could never 'make love' – has been preying on my mind and in my imagination. The next time I go to Spain and find myself making love to a Flamenco dancer by the fountains of the Alhambra will she dampen my passion by suddenly saying, 'By the way, I am a Basque Separatist'? I wonder, and I also go on wondering about the Woolwich train. Our fantasist was recently joined by two young gay men who got into his carriage when it made the first stop on the way to Charing Cross. He claims they asked him, 'Do you mind if we make love?' He says he replied, 'I don't mind what you do as long as you don't smoke.' When the train arrived at the terminus he says they adjusted their dress and said, 'Thank you sir, you're a gentleman.' So he tells us, and should a trip to Woolwich ever arise I shall take a mini-cab and enough money for 16 large vodkas. Lager is so patronising.

Anyway, he is now having an affair with a Filipino au pair girl and claims that he is giving her mother one on the side as well. We await, in the Coach and Horses, with bated breath to hear of their political affiliations. I also await with bated eyes to see if he walks into the Coach minus his ears when the mother finds out. What a dull life I have led. It is true that I was once in bed with a girl who suddenly announced that Charles Dickens was a fascist, but she had irrepressible opinions on everything and I carried on as though nothing had happened. Nothing much does happen to me nowadays. Our man in Woolwich is doing all the dreaming for us. But still, I can't help wondering what it would be like to be in bed with 15 black, gay Tories all drinking lager and at my expense. No doubt we shall hear any day now.

14 December 1985

INTENSIVE CARE

MATERNITY

A SOHO CHARACTER

A couple of Sundays ago I was watching *Songs of Praise*, which was coming from Maidstone Prison of all places, when to my amazement I spotted a man in the congregation of the chapel who owes me £50. He was standing there and had the gall to be singing 'Abide With Me'. I know that none of us are beyond redemption, although the vicar of Chaddleworth in Berkshire once told me that he thought I was, but I thought it was a bit of a bloody nerve in a strange way. It further struck me that he was probably a 'trusty', in which case all I can say is that the prison governor had better hang on to his wallet if he happens to interview Jimmy. I wouldn't swear to it but when it came to the last line of the chorus, 'Lord with me abide', I think Jimmy was singing, 'I'll take you for a ride'. I would have gone out to a restaurant that evening too if I'd had an extra 50 quid. Oh well, you can't win 'em all, and that, I'm afraid, reminds me that yet another of our Soho mates, Frank Blake, died last week.

The fact that someone is 74, smokes 60 cigarettes a day and drinks doesn't alter the fact that it's sad when a man dies. You want them to hang on for a little longer. Frank was a man who happened to be a terrible nuisance in a way with his nonsenses about being what he called a 'Soho character'. Nevertheless he made a sort of benign impact on the place. His family were a strange mixture. He was a fairly rough-sounding cockney with a fighting background and yet his brother was a Jesuit priest in Farm Street. Frank was best known as a master of ceremonies at wrestling fights and was often seen on television in that capacity. We first got to know each other years ago when I was navvying and laying the foundations of Kemble House, the block of flats opposite the French pub. Near the end of every week, penniless, I'd go up to his appalling flat in Old Compton Street and pawn something with him, usually a fountain pen, to raise 10 shillings. He loved it. It made him feel like something out of Charles Dickens.

The flat was quite something. It stands at the top of 72 steps and that might have helped kill him. It was a snip at about £2 a week, but, as I say, it was pretty ropey. He had to boil a kettle to wash or shave. He had a pay-phone on the wall along with a photograph of himself shaking hands with the Duke of Edinburgh at some fight function and he had a laugh that could have stemmed from a hysterical dog. We spent many hours in the old snooker club in Frith Street where Bunny May swept all before him at snooker and Frank would play kaluki, a form of rummy, with an assorted bunch of villains. In his more recent days he would bemoan, along with a lot of us, the decline of Soho. He would stop me in the street and with the face of someone who was lost would say, 'But where have all the characters gone?' He seemed quite bewildered at what time, the declining quality of life and Lord Wolfenden's wretched report had done to his little village. He used to appear in the Patisserie Valerie, above which he lived, every morning to get two bread rolls. The appearances were made in pyjamas covered by a pretty disgusting raincoat. And he always wore bedroom slippers. What he should have done was to have a more comfortable life. He had the money to get a flat with running hot water, he collected sovereigns which became devalued, but he was glued to Soho, a fairly common but chronic attachment some of us formed. There is no known cure for it except for the road to Golders Green.

Well, there's not many of us left. I was totting up deaths and obituaries the other day and it is rather depressing but inevitable I suppose once you hit 50. It isn't Soho characters I miss so much as contemporaries. You find yourself looking around and wondering who's next. You avoid the looking glass except for necessities. One of the ways in which I shall miss Frank is that such people are a 'connection'. Not just to life as one is used to it, but to the past and simply being. Frank's biggest laugh was when I, desperate for £8, sparred a couple of rounds with Sandy Saddler, the featherweight champion of the world, and got damn nigh killed. I can hear that laugh now. It is a terrible sound.

8 March 1986

JOHN BETJEMAN

CITY AND SUBURBAN

Clichés

'Excuse me,' said a lady to me when I was crossing Hammersmith Broadway. She elbowed me off the traffic island and asserted her rights on the zebra crossing in front of a bus. When people say 'Excuse me' I always reply 'No,' and they look round, as this lady did, risking her life in doing so, in pained amazement. 'Excuse me' is only one of the phrases current today which has lost its original meaning. Today it means 'Get out of the way.' 'Can I help you, sir?' means 'What the hell are you doing here?' 'With due respect' or 'In all respect' means 'I have no respect for your opinions at all.' For years now 'To be frank' has meant 'To be unpardonably rude.' As our language loses its meaning (a Post Office official told a friend of mine the other day that he would 'organise' a telephone for him), so local accents disappear and clichés take their place. There is technological jargon, education jargon, church jargon and so on.

I was in Bristol on Sunday exploring Kingsdown, a leafy Georgian suburb of cobbled lanes, steps, pear trees and bow-windowed houses, all threatened with destruction on an airy hilltop in that wonderful city. But I listened in vain as I talked to people for the intrusive liquid which used to be a feature of that part of Bristol. Ernest Bevin had it. He used to pu 'l's on to words ending with an 'a' or an 'o' – 'idea-l,' 'banana-l'; and, of course, 'Bristol' was originally 'Bristowe.' But there is still in the City of London, among older brokers and company directors, that delightful thing the 'City accent' which went with an Italianate house with a gravel drive and lamp posts in Streatham or Lewisham and has now migrated to Esher and Sussex. The vowels are rather broad and flat. The speech is slow and shrewdly thoughtful.

4 October 1957

Religious Revival

The lastest craze among Teddy boys is for jangling with holy medals and even crucifixes. A friend of mine who works in the East End asked a Teddy boy who was wearing a medal of St Christopher what its significance was. 'I don't know,' he said. 'It is of an old man carrying a kid. But we all have to wear them. We must be in the fashion.'

11 October 1957

A New County

I hear a nasty rumour that some merciless administrators are trying to unite the Soke of Peterborough and the Isle of Ely into one new county. It is a most inhuman idea, for the two places have disliked one another since the days of Hereward the Wake. The Isle was separate from Cambridgeshire until 1836 and still has its own courts and local government officers. The Soke, though it is much smaller, and for some curious reason coloured the same as Northamptonshire on the maps, is even more proudly independent. The late Lord Exeter was Lord Paramount or Custos Rotulorum of the Soke acting under a commission of oyer and terminer. He appointed the magistrates who, I believe, still retain the power of hanging a criminal for murder and exercised it as late as 1812. I was in the Soke in the golden sunlight of last Saturday on behalf of the Friends of Peterborough Cathedral, that grand building whose west front is surely one of the most beautiful mediæval compositions in Europe. I came by train from Bridge Street, Northampton, through the gentle Nene Valley. The bigger stations such as Bridge Street, Irthlingborough, Wellingborough and Oundle are like 1840 Tudor parsonage houses. The yellowing willows, the oaks and elms still green, the towers and spires of churches on hill slopes, old limestone cottages and farms variegated with bands of ironstone, all confirmed my impression that Northamptonshire is one of the most beautiful as it is one of the least regarded counties in England. But once we were through the tunnel at Wansford and into the Soke, we were in another country which partook of East Anglia and not of the Midlands. Some remarks that the Soke ought to be an independent country like San Marino drew forth applause and cries of 'We are proud of it!' And this is no joke. Local pride, separate regiments, separate local government, separate courts and old customs are essential to English life. We are driven into big groups, but we are happier in small ones. Local rivalry built the towers and spires of England when village vied with village. Who in Ely wants to pay his electricity bill in Peterborough and who in the Soke wants to pay for Chatteris, Wisbech and March? And why should one county have two of the best English cathedrals?

18 October 1957

Authors

Many authors, when one meets them for the first time, are comparatively unimpressive compared with their books. But Lord Dunsany, who died last week, never disappointed. He was every inch a poet, playwright, storyteller, Irish peer, big-game hunter, painter, modeller in clay, Conservative politician, soldier and country gentleman, all of which occupations he followed in the busiest and most-enjoyed life I have seen. He was a tall, splendid-looking man with a young voice, decided opinions and boundless energy. He was very happily married and had the good manners of an Edwardian autocrat. Unexpected things roused his anger. One of them was manufactured salt in advertised brands (he mistrusted everything that was branded and advertised) – if he found this on a dinner table, no matter whose house it was, he would say, 'Send for some ordinary kitchen salt and bring two glasses of water.' He would then pour some of the branded salt into one glass and the kitchen salt into another. The kitchen salt dissolved, but the branded salt left a white deposit at the bottom of the other glass which he said was either chalk or ground-up bones. He was one of those people who made you feel on top of the world and that

"Give us a quid!"

all those who disagreed with you were petty crooks who would be beaten in the end. He talked with all the fantasy of his own Jorkens stories.

Throwing up the ball

Another author who never disappoints when one meets him is Sir Compton Mackenzie. I think this is becaue his approach to strangers is the other way round to that of most people. He is prejudiced in their favour, whatever they might have done in the past, until they say or do something in his presence which damns them. I remember him once telling me that he did not regard himself as a literary man but as an entertainer, as he came from a family of entertainers. And he entertained me last week in Edinburgh with an example of Henry James's conversation which I will find it difficult to put into words.

James was criticising Mackenzie's novel *Carnival* to him, saying that perhaps the lady delineated in that book was too delicately modelled for the vast structure in which she was set, and ending, 'but then I said the same to Flaubert about *Madame Bovary*.' Mackenzie, flattered, said that he was intending to rewrite the book. 'Never do that,' said James, 'I have wasted twelve precious years of my life doing such things. You are the one member of your generation who can throw up the ball and receive it back into his hands. But when I throw up the ball it hits first one wall, bounces to another and then another, until it finally rolls slowly to my feet and with my aching, ageing limbs I struggle to bend down and pick it up.' He told me that James used to send résumés of his novels before he wrote them to his agent Pinker and that these were marvellous short stories. I wonder what has become of them.

1 November 1957

URSULA BUCHAN

AGONY AUNT

This month, having run out of ideas of my own, I answer some readers' letters.

We have some hard landscape in our gardens which consists of a series of stone steps down which water flows in a cascade. We are worried that algae growth may build up.
S.D.P., Chatsworth, Derbyshire

I'm afraid you don't tell me how big the waterfall is or how much time you can spend in the garden (or, indeed, whether you are lucky enough to have any help). Can I suggest that once a year you turn the water off and give the steps a really good scrub with a stiff brush and some diluted household bleach? You'll need to use some elbow-grease! I wonder if you've considered covering these steps with a length of blue butyl pond liner? You can get it these days at most garden centres. That way your waterfall will be easier to maintain and could become a real feature in your garden!

I've got a plant which was given to me for my birthday; it is in a pot; it may have had flowers but I can't remember seeing any and the leaves have all turned brown and dropped off. Have I over-watered it?
A.W.A., Spalding, Lincs.

The plant you describe is quite obviously *Dieffenbachia picta*, which was introduced from Brazil in 1820. It is a tropical plant which requires a minimum winter temperature of 16°C (61°F). It has dark green ovate leaves, blotched with white, and these easily go brown and die off in dry conditions. So retain high humidity at all times, without over-watering, by standing the pot on a tray of pebbles which can be topped up with water.

West Indian plantation owners used to give the leaves of this plant to recalcitrant slaves whose mouths, when they ate it, would swell up painfully (hence its nickname 'Dumb Cane'). Don't, however, give it to the *au pair* or she'll never finish that language course!

Can you recommend a really good spray to deal with greenfly?

R.B., Bracknell

Alas, not yet. But I live in hope that a chemical company may one day offer a sufficiently large retainer for me to do so with complete confidence.

I was having an argument with my neighbour over the fence last night. He is adamant that Canadian pondweed, Elodea canadensis, *is an example of agamospermic reproduction. I maintain it is just good, old-fashioned apomixis. Surely it couldn't be cleistogamy, could it? What do you think?*

D.B., Durham

It all depends on what you mean by agamospermy.

When we moved here, we found that part of the garden contained nothing but plants which are white. What can you suggest to turn this drab corner into a really lovely splash of colour?

N.T., Sissinghurst, Kent

Well, don't some people have extraordinary ideas! And the oddest gardening opinions always seem to be held by anyone from whom one buys a house! Fortunately, your problem is easily put right – just think yourself lucky that you haven't been saddled with some unsightly permanent feature (say, a huge brick tower) in the middle of your garden! May I recommend what I like to call my 'Bobbydazzler Selection', which is guaranteed to brighten up the dullest spot? Throw out all those dreary white tobacco plants and Madonna lilies, and replace them with a smashing mixture of busy Lizzies (like *Impatiens* 'Novette' in deep orange, scarlet-red, salmon, white and rose), some of the new, fringed, double petunias and lots 'n lots of

You're being deliberately provocative.

colourful Giant Cactus-Flowered zinnias. That's sure to create a sensation should you have any visitors. But don't go too far. Restraint can be a virtue in gardening. Why not keep the hostas?

I have a back garden which is shaded by a large sycamore tree in the next-door garden. The soil is a mixture of light stony brash, yellow subsoil and dried-up cement which the builders left. All the local cats use it as a public convenience and water drips from an upstairs overflow on to it, turning it into concrete in summer and a mud morass in winter. I should like to grow colourful hardy flowers in it for 12 months of the year, in a simple, tasteful, harmony of pinks, blues and greys. It should not cost much to plant up, should last without alteration for years and years, and must be labour-saving. What can you suggest?

E.B., Clapham

Nothing.

What is the Fibonacci series?

U.B., Northants

I could not even begin to guess. Anyway, it is very bad form, even if you haven't received enough letters, to write to yourself. Look it up.

Miss Buchan regrets that she is far too idle to enter into private correspondence.

29 August 1987

ANTHONY DANIELS

THE DOCTOR'S DILEMMA

The first time I told someone that their closest relative was soon to die, I felt the seductive thrill of power. It did not occur to me that actually it was an admission of impotence in the face of nature; nor that it was an outrage that a junior medical student like myself should be deputed to pass on this most delicate of messages, on the grounds that everyone else was far too busy to do it. I enjoyed for once being a person of the utmost significance.

My moment of glory, as it happens, was ruined by the fact that the woman whose husband was about to die was nearly stone deaf.

'I'm afraid I have some bad news for you,' I said importantly. 'Your husband is very ill and there is no chance of recovery.'

She looked at me without any change in her expression whatsoever. She's taking this very calmly, I thought, somewhat deflated by my apparent lack of impact.

'Mum's deaf,' said her teenage daughter who was sitting beside her.

I repeated my message in a raised voice, and finally shouted it, until the whole ward vibrated. The technical difficulty of transmitting the message had by now far transcended in importance its content.

The daughter put her face close to her mother's and spoke very distinctly so that her mother could lip-read.

'The doctor says Dad's going to die soon.'

'Oh,' said the mother, 'I wondered what he was trying to tell me.'

One soon learns in medicine that, whatever philosophers may say, truth is a slippery concept, is not always desirable, and that my truth is not necessarily your truth. Those who demand between doctor and patient absolute and unvarying frankness – the truth, the whole truth, and nothing but the truth, as it were – must have a very simple view of social relations.

There are, of course, many ways of softening the blows of an unkind world. I knew of one doctor who conceived it his duty always to tell the patient about his disease.

'Well, Mr Jones,' he said, 'you haven't got cancer.'

'Oh good,' said Mr Jones, looking up weak and helpless from his bed.

'And you haven't got leukaemia.'

'Oh good,' said Mr Jones.

'No,' said the doctor, 'you've got something in between the two.'

My own efforts to reduce suffering by presenting another side of reality have not met with uniform success. As a student I once found a woman who was about to have an operation weeping in her bed in a surgical ward. I asked her why.

'They think I've got cancer,' she said. 'They might cut my bosom off.'

I sought to console her. The surgeon, I said, was an excellent man, careful and technically sound. We should relieve any pain she felt after the operation, and it would soon be over. She had nothing to worry about: the surgeon had performed hundreds of these operations before. She burst into further floods of tears.

'But I've only got two!' she said.

There is, however, one particular truth that very few patients can accept: namely, that there is nothing a doctor can do for them.

I was once on duty in a hospital when a woman in her early sixties with absurdly jet-black hair, heavily made-up and with little golden Maltese crosses dangling from her ear-lobes, came with her husband following meekly behind her.

'Doctor, can you lock him up?' she asked.

'For how long would you like us to lock him up?' I inquired.

'The rest of his life, of course,' she said. 'He's dangerous.'

He didn't look dangerous to me, but you never can tell.

'He's just tried to kill me,' she said.

'How?' I asked.

'He fetched a crowbar to me.'

Her appearance may have been peculiar, but it had not been arranged by a crowbar.

'I hope you'll excuse my asking,' I said, 'but if your husband

has just attacked you with a crowbar, how come you are not
dead – or even marked?'

She evidently considered my question naive.

'I set the dog on him, of course.'

The dog was a Dobermann specially trained to attack her
husband at her word of command. Her husband, it seemed,
tried to murder her once or twice a decade. They had been
married for nearly 40 years.

'Is all this true?' I asked, turning to the husband.

'Yes,' he replied. 'You see, doctor, it's like this . . .'

He explained that he was the caretaker of a large bank
building.

'And when I come home of an evening, all I want to do is sit
and relax with the evening paper. But she,' he said, pointing to
his wife, who was shaking with indignation, 'wants to talk.
That's all she does: talk, talk, talk. And when she talks, them
earrings – they go jiggle, jiggle, jiggle. I just couldn't stand it no
more, doctor, so I came home with this crowbar.'

I looked at her earrings and saw his point.

'What are you going to do about him?' asked his wife.

'There's nothing I *can* do about him.'

'There must be. I mean, he's just tried to kill me, and you're a
doctor.'

'You can try the police,' I suggested.

'But I mean, if he tries to kill me, he must be sick in the head.'

'It by no means follows,' I said.

'He may try to kill me again.'

'He may,' I agreed. 'In fact, I think it is likely.'

'Can't you lock him up to prevent him?'

I quoted the 18th-century judge, Lord Mansfield.

'As long as an act remains in bare intention alone, it is not
punishable by our law.'

'You're a funny doctor,' she said.

'I'm afraid you must take the decision yourself: either you
stay with your husband and risk being murdered, or you leave
him and face the resulting difficulties. Doctors cannot help
you.'

'Come on Henry,' she said to her crowbar-toting husband.
'Let's go.' Henry followed her meekly out of the door. 'He
can't help us.'

As Billy Bunter once translated a famous Latin aphorism, great is the truth, and it will prevail a bit.

28 July 1984

WILLIAM DEEDES

MY EVENING WITH IMELDA

A pity Charles Moore in his Diary last week snitched a silver teaspoon off the table at which I dined with Imelda Marcos late last summer. But it was a well-laden table – silver guilt, actually – and now that they have looted the Malacanang Palace and Imelda has gone into exile it bears a return visit. A fragment of the past, it can never happen again.

Moore says I made an 'uncharacteristic mistake' in telling Mrs Marcos there should be a musical made of her on the lines of *Evita*. (To which she wittily replied: 'I didn't start life as a prostitute!') In mitigation, the evening with her had then lasted over four hours, during which she had barely drawn breath. It was essential to say *something* – and it was no good saying 'goodbye'.

Our man in Manila who with his wife was one of the seven round our table had tried that. At midnight, as to the manner born, he pushed his chair back a shade and murmured: 'First Lady, this has been a memorable evening. . . .' Forty minutes later, we were still at the table, and an unseen pianist was still giving us a beautiful distant accompaniment.

Lest one seems to be giving oneself airs, it is necessary to explain why this dinner took place. Serious Americans, in ascending order of proximity to President Reagan, had been swooping into Manila all summer. Their futile mission was to persuade Marcos to sort himself out.

Accompanied by the blessed Ian Ward of the *Daily Telegraph*, experienced in all Pacific affairs, I had ventured there because 'sources' had told me that these unknown people in a far-off land might be about to explode, with serious global consequences. An aimless English editor must have appeared to Ferdinand Marcos (who also afforded me a long talk) and his wife relief from the Washington arm-twisters. We were welcomed. The first dinner date she offered us, indeed, unluckily clashed with an evening we had arranged with the opposition. Surprisingly, she was free the next night as well.

The dinner party began strangely. Ward and I were at first left totally alone to pace the enormous gallery of the Palace in which hung portraits of earlier presidents. There we were joined by a handsome and intelligent lady-in-waiting, one of the Blue Ladies as they were called, Carmen Nakpil, mother of the first Filipino beauty queen. I say she was intelligent because almost the first thing she did was to offer us a drink. She rang a bell and ordered whiskies. Alas, at that very moment doors were flung open, lights blazed and we were summoned into the presence.

I was placed on a sofa beside Imelda Marcos, but without my drink. The television crews and lighting men outnumbered the guests. It had been a terrible year, she said; drought, the floods, financial difficulties, the Americans, her husband's illness – and the killing of Aquino. 'A political disaster,' she said looking me in the eye.

Dazzled and thirsty – the whiskies arrived 20 minutes later – I did not find it easy to keep up with this line of small talk. At most dinner parties I go to there is banter over drinks, more serious talk at the table. Mrs Marcos reversed this convention. For 45 minutes she provided, over my single whisky, a comprehensive briefing on her country's difficulties, its history and its place in the world; its large Catholic community – 'but only two cardinals'; and finally world strategy in the Pacific and South China Sea. Not once was she at loss for a figure or a fact.

When we eventually got to the laden dinner table – five courses, four wines – she relaxed and turned to the story of her life. One of 11 children, and all of them had played a different musical instrument. Imagine! Her mother had been a singer. She had agreed to marry Marcos without her father's consent; or rather, when Marcos popped the question there was no telephone at hand.

Their early married life had been frugal – only 300 pesos a week – and Marcos had jibbed after six weeks at finding that she was spending nearly half the housekeeping on flowers. This was necessary, she reassured him, because their love must be surrounded by beauty. She spoke at great length and quite unselfconsciously about beauty in the world and its spiritual values. Once or twice, listening to this astonishing figure in her short black silk frock, adorned by a single jewel and a snatch of bright silk at the throat, I pinched myself to make sure it was not a dream, something few of us have done since childhood.

She spoke of her aunt. General MacArthur had been in love with her – his marriage (she said) had not worked out. Once as a child, shortly after the General had fulfilled his vow to return, she had leaned from an upstairs window and seen her aunt and MacArthur on the beach below clutched in passionate embrace. The aunt never married, she said, and had died a month after MacArthur. The tale was told in a style which made the story of Antony and Cleopatra seen mundane.

Then she spoke of her encounters with Colonel Gaddafi, whom she found 'macho'. 'You seem a reasonable woman,' he had told her, and he begged her to embrace the Muslim faith. He had given her a marked copy of the Koran, and then sent her a dozen copies. She had been going to do an oil deal with him, but royalty in the Gulf had talked her out of it. Gaddafi had also sent her a romantic telegram; but when alone with him her line had always been: 'You are a good man, a religious man.' Although he was 'very macho' that had kept him at bay.

She had told Vice-President Bush of these adventures and he had asked Casey of the CIA to debrief her about them. This took four hours. Then the inevitable question had to be asked: 'Did you actually sleep with Colonel Gaddafi?' 'What a question to ask a girl,' exclaimed Mrs Marcos gaily at our dinner table.

And then, at a different level, there was the story of the school chum who failed all her examinations. One day Mrs Marcos had met her in the Vatican. 'Where do you live now?' 'Here.' 'Here – but what do you do?' The school friend was engaged, said Imelda, in beautiful needlework for the Pope. So her friend had found perfect fulfilment, and this went to prove that all human beings are of equal value. By then the seventh member at our table, a general, deputy Governor (to Mrs Marcos) of Metro Manila, was fast asleep at the table, but silently and unobtrusively so. Perhaps he had heard some of it before.

As we finally took leave of Mrs Marcos, long past midnight, in the drawing room, my eye took one last look at the massed flowers, the countless signed portraits of the international greats – only Princess Margaret from our quarter – and the weary television crew, I gave myself another pinch. Looking at her, I saw no trace of fatigue, the eyes still bright, the complexion fresh, the pile of dark hair on her head still faultlessly arranged.

'I feel indebted to you for an unusual experience,' our Ambassador said to me as we awaited our cars in the palace forecourt. 'Not one we are likely to repeat in our lifetime, Excellency,' I replied. No, indeed.

8 March 1986

'This is a recording. I'm sorry you're at the end of your tether – if you could put off committing suicide for 24 hours, somebody will be here to attend to you'.

ALICE THOMAS ELLIS

FOOT FAULT

I bought some comfortable shoes the other day: white moccasin-type things with fringed tongues, and flat as a pancake. Alfie hates them to such an extent that he has become quite unbalanced on the subject. Whenever we meet his eyes go straight to my feet and, should I happen to be wearing them, he starts clawing at the air and invoking the Deity. 'You look like a Third World person,' he says. 'You look as though you'd found them on a tip where another Third World person had thrown them away. You look like a *Peruvian*,' he adds despairingly. He says the very sight of them makes him go all limp and *leffargic* and puts him off his lunch and the prospect of work and, by implication, the whole of the human race. Alfie is very sensitive. He sank to the floor the other day, moaning about my shoes. He says he wouldn't mind so much if they were only black and, if I would just go and buy a bottle of dye (he was too weak to move) he would paint them for me. I sometimes find people's hats unbearably annoying, but I can't remember shoes having this effect on me.

I'm still feeling pretty leffargic myself. I've been explaining to everyone that the cold was rendering me incapable of all forms of work, but when the sun came out last Sunday I didn't feel galvanised a bit. The other day, in the house of my friend the analyst, where I go to work, I was overwhelmed by weariness and went to sleep instead, sharing my couch with the cat Focus who, his master says, has to have a kip in the afternoon in order to get into shape for the night's sleep. But then all the cats I know get up at 5 a.m. and clump around wondering when the lazy bastards are going to wake and give them their breakfast. Cadders and Puss stand outside the bathroom going miaow and occasionally slapping and scratching at the door. Their importunity quite spoils one's concentration as one lies in the bath plotting a novel and listening to Ken Bruce on the wireless.

Sometimes a black snake-like paw insinuates itself under the door and you feel like someone in a James Bond movie where naked people are always being menaced by reptiles and tarantulas and odd-looking foreign chaps.

The daughter and I are taking an unprecedented Easter break and leaving the rest of the family to cook their own Easter bunny. We are going to Scotland and it has just dawned on me that this involves sitting in a car for 14 hours. I never recognise unpleasant facts until I can see the whites of their eyes, but this one is doing nothing for my metabolic rate. We are travelling over night and I'm tired already. What car games can one play with a child in total darkness? We shall have to tell jokes: 'What do you call a nun with a washing machine on her head? 'Sister Matic.' 'Why are elephants grey and wrinkled and huge?' 'Because if they were little and round and white they'd be aspirins.' She knows some very rude ones too but I'll spare you those. I have toyed with the idea of asking a vet for a few tranquillising darts but I suppose we will have to rely on a plentiful supply of Smarties. I do detest travelling.

We have been instructed to bring the minimum of luggage to the Isle of Arran since the car is alarmingly minute, and this means heart-rending decisions, together with shrewd predictions as to what the weather will be doing – always problematic at this time of year. Is it worse to have only tweeds and great hairy woollies when the sun beams from a cloudless sky, or only pretty little cotton frocks while the north-easterlies roar in from the ocean? One thing is sure. I'm taking my comfortable white shoes, and sucks to you Alfie.
PS: I shouldn't have written that because Alfie has just walked in, peered under the table to ascertain what I've got on my feet and gone completely mad: 'Get those effing shoes off,' he said. 'They make you look like ten bob's worth down King's Cross.' Then he tore them from my feet and put them in the bin liner.

29 March 1986

PIG TALES

Someone is thrilled to bits with his latest publication. It is entitled *The History of the British Pig* and is by Julian Wiseman and I have to confess that, for reasons I cannot precisely put my finger on, it *is* rather compelling. I have never previously given much thought to the pig, being aware of him only as a balding pink creature with a curly tail, teetering around in muck on little high-heeled hooves. I have rubbed oil and salt into his skin to make his crackling crisp, and I have grown as annoyed as everyone else to find that the manufacturers have somehow contrived to introduce a great deal of water into his bacon so that it sticks to the pan which consequently has to be scoured before you can fry the eggs in it. I have also retained in my mind for years a piece of probably untrue, and certainly useless, information to the effect that chocolate is poison to pigs and if found in their swill will cause them to drop down dead. As I detest waste I was cross to learn some years ago of the abandonment of the scheme whereby what people left on their plates in various canteens and institutions was scraped into bins to be converted into swill for these omnivorous animals. I used to worry vaguely sometimes, when I couldn't think of anything else to worry about, that the remains of a Mars bar or a cup of cocoa might inadvertently be included by some ignorant person and cause mayhem in the piggeries. I knew like everyone else that every bit of the pig, apart from the squeak, was of use to mankind, and I have heard that it is very painful to be bitten by one. But then being bitten by anything isn't very nice. Apart from all that I was content to let the pig go his way while I went mine. No longer. The pig is a peculiarly fascinating beast, and now that I have broken my silence on the subject I have been astonished at the numbers of people who have long held this view.

Wherein then lies the appeal? Perhaps, I muse, it arises from the ambivalence which mankind feels towards this animal. In the introduction to *The History of the British Pig* the author quotes one John Mills as follows: 'Of all the quadrupeds that we know, or at least certainly of all those that come under the husbandman's care, the Hog appears to be the foulest, the most brutish, and the most apt to commit waste wherever it goes. The defects of its figure seems to influence its dispositions: all its ways are gross, all its inclinations are filthy, and all its sensations concentrate in a furious lust, and so eager a gluttony, that it devours indiscriminately whatever comes its way.' Help. It seems particularly unfair to cast aspersions on the pig's figure, since an illustration of the common pig of Europe shows him to be as slim as you could wish and it is undoubtedly the hand of man that has fattened the hog. Having devoured *The History* of same I looked eagerly round for further reading and was handed by Someone *The Book of the Pig*, a 19th-century work crammed with the misleading scientific information so dear to the Victorians, and full of the most amazing pictures – some of which also appear in the book under discussion. I particularly recommend the drawing of two Poland Chinas; they are *all* solid pig with teensy little snouts and weensy little legs and look exactly like two dirigibles – as remote from the wild boar as the Pomeranian from the wolf. Then there is the print dated 1809 showing a chap in a hat with a sow about ten times his size. Artistic licence, you think to yourself. But no. There it is in black and white: 'This pig weighed 12 cwt at four years of age.' Below that is a picture of a practically circular pig which, observes the author, was, at 802 lbs live weight, by no means the largest recorded. He isn't kidding. Turning to my other source I read that 'in America . . . a hog was exhibited which reached the marvellous weight of 1325 lb'. That is one hell of a lot of pork chops. By this time the gentry had taken over the breeding of the pig. Left to himself and without the help of such as Lord Emsworth, the peasant would have been content with his little pig of no particular breed rootling round in his backyard, or foraging in the woods (this was called pannage and the peasant had to pay for it). Now we have all sorts of pigs – black, white, mottled, spotted, saddled, sheeted, razor-backed, lop-eared, everything the heart could desire. At least I think we have. Some of them might have died out again and I haven't seen a live one for ages except at a distance. Now that my interest has been kindled I am determined to make closer acquaintance with this underrated beast.

3 May 1986

PETER FLEMING (STRIX)

THE SPINACH-SPIES OF PORTLAND PLACE

'I want some meat.'

'Yes, sir,' said the butcher. I could see that he expected me to particularise. His small shop was festooned with meat. It would have been better to have been more specific in the first place.

I asked for cutlets. From a planning point of view the cutlet is an easy unit to deal with. Start dabbling in technicalities like tenderloins and saddles and briskets and you may find yourself bulk-purchasing and finish up with enough food for a fortnight.

'Family away?' asked the butcher's wife in a faintly compassionate tone while her husband got to work with his chopper.

'Yes,' I said.

Because two Labradors normally travel in my car, I always put the meat in the boot, I then forget all about it and have spaghetti for luncheon because Inge, the Danish cook, assumes that I have omitted to order any meat. I thus prove to be an economical housekeeper.

I am, however, overwhelmed by a sense of my inadequacy in this role when I listen to *Shopping List,* a five-minute programme which the BBC puts out twice a week at 8.15 a.m. It consists of what staff officers would call a sitrep on food, and is read by the announcer. It seeks to have superseded a similar programme called *Shopping Flash.* This was read, in rotation, by a small team of rather effusive ladies; it was chatty and personal ('there's more than a hint of autumn round the corner when you find apples tumbling into season'). I always switched it off.

The new programme, on the other hand, exerts a curious fascination on me. This is partly because of announcer-participation. When I hear those grave mellifluous, demi-official tones exhorting us 'when choosing cucumbers, look to see they are firm,' or suggesting that 'if your fishmonger sells double fillets of haddock, these will probably be cheaper per pound than the single fillets,' I become sharply aware of what a many-faceted business one man's life can be. I find something piquant in the fact that the voice which ten minues ago was appraising us of portentous events, telling us of disasters and detonations and Mr Dulles, is now, in exactly the same well-modulated accents, revealing that 'cauliflowers have had particular recommendation in the Glasgow area'. There is a faint but unmistakable note of parody about the whole thing which I like very much.

Brief and impersonal though it is, the transmission opens up – or, rather, affords a glimpse of – a new, an unfamiliar, a challenging world. It is a world in which I myself would soon get lost. 'Flake,' said the BBC on August 9, 'should be cheaper than it has been recently.' I do not know what flake is.* Textual evidence suggests that it is some sort of fish, but were I to inquire the price of a pound of it (or should it be a pound of *them*? Perhaps flake are tiny little creatures, like whitebait) how could I possibly tell whether the price quoted was lower than it had been recently? I should be a mere gull, at the mercy of an unscrupulous fishmonger.

'Seventeen and six?' I would quaver. 'Isn't that rather a *lot* for a pound? The BBC said –'

'Seventeen and six a lot for a pound of *flake*!' the fishmonger would roar indignantly. 'Come, come, sir! You'll be telling me I don't know my own business next.'

And I would pay up, blushing and muttering apologies. A great pale hunk of fish would join the spare wheel and the grouse-feathers in the oubliette.

I immensely admire the assurance with which the BBC picks its way, unerring and authoritative, about this strange, still-life, cornucopian world, judiciously quizzing the saithe and the persimmons, the bilberries and the chicken halibut (is this an old trade name for flying fish?). How do they do it? What are their sources of information?

You have only to listen to the stuff they transmit to realise that its collation and assessment must be the work of an intelligence service, and a highly organised one at that.

* The BBC may have said 'hake'; but the word appears, *passim*, as 'flake' in the scripts which my ubiquitous agents have procured for me.

However casually the announcer may make them, statements like 'Dover soles are recommended, and there is *some good quality line-caught halibut*' reflect an advanced standard of training among the BBC's food-spies. As, turning up their coat collars, they pause to light an unobtrusive cigarette in front of the fishmonger's slab, can they tell by the expression on the halibut's lifeless face that it was caught on a line and not in a net? I suppose they must be able to.

'In several areas small Queen pineapples are inexpensive.' What a lot of travelling they must do to obtain even so trivial an item of intelligence! And, if it comes to that, what a lot of eating, or at least nibbling! 'The straight, perfectly formed beans are more expensive, but the flavouring of *all* is good.' My italics, but they miss nothing. 'There are some globe artichokes in the Bristol area. . . . Some cherries are split. . . . Prawns are in first-class condition. . . . Shoppers are advised to look for filleted codling.'

It is bootless and might be indiscreet to speculate too closely about the methods by which the BBC has built up this nation-wide spy-ring; but no one can listen to its terse, oracular reports without feeling admiration for the anonymous men and women who have spent the previous day scurrying from counter to counter, prodding flounders, pinching pears, counting radishes and noting the price of gammon.

Are there ever any repercussions? I have noticed, for instance, that cheese is never mentioned. No doubt there is some good reason for this, but has no irate deputation from the National Association of Cheesemakers ever demanded to know what it is? And is the BBC being fair to fishmongers when it gives the public advice on how to get a bargain in haddock?

Finally, how on earth did shoppers *manage* in the days before wireless, when they could not listen for five minutes twice a week to an urbane voice telling them that 'Pickled brisket is a little dearer than the forequarter flank'? This small, beneficent BBC programme supplies – to borrow a diagnosis applied over several decades by the great Beachcomber to the pullulating amenities of our society – proof (if proof were needed) that we are not living in the Middle Ages.

27 September 1957

THE OTHERNESS OF SNEED

I suppose that in almost every club there is a member who, though he uses the place a great deal, never really seems to *belong*. He is not exactly aloof; he is not mysterious; he does not give the impression of being shy. He is rather like the lizard on the wall of your bungalow in the tropics. Spread-eagled, brooding, inscrutable and vaguely proprietorial, liable at any moment to vanish none can say whither, to reappear none can say whence, the lizard produces a disturbing sensation of *otherness*; and it is rather the same with the type of member I have in mind.

There is one at the Culverin Club. I think his name is Sneed; I have always thought this. But I once heard him addressed as Fortescue by a member whom I do not know. 'Good morning, Fortescue,' said this chap as they passed each other in a doorway. 'Good morning,' replied (as I maintain) Sneed in a flat, ungracious voice; from the quick appraising glance which he gave the other you could deduce nothing. There was perhaps a flicker of surprise in it, but no more than you would expect from a man who, since he never speaks to anybody, is virtually never spoken to himself.

Most of us, if addressed *en passant* by the wrong name, tend to react in some positive way. We look blank, taken aback. We begin (even if we only begin) to expostulate by saying 'Er' or 'What?' or 'As a matter of fact.' We join a group of acquaintances and ask if anybody knows the tall man in glasses who has just left the room and who appears to believe that our name is Smethurst. We *do* something about it.

The fact that Sneed did nothing throws, in my view, no light on what his name really is. This aura of otherness, this highly-developed capacity for appearing not to belong, are perfectly compatible with the acceptance of an alias, fortuitously bestowed. It is of course possible that Fortescue is Sneed's Christian name; but the inherent improbability of anybody calling Sneed by his Christian name is so great that I think we can rule out this solution.

It must be five years or more since an incident occurred in which Sneed's behaviour became, for the first and as far as I know the last time, positively rather than negatively enigmatic.

The other person involved was Dinmont, the distinguished actor. One morning he and Sneed were sitting opposite each other on either side of the fireplace in the reading room, looking through the illustrated papers. At one o'clock or thereabouts Dinmont got up to go into luncheon. As he did so Sneed put down the *Tatler*, directed at his fellow-member a searching glance, and spoke.

'I see,' he said, 'that you've put your socks on today, Dinmont.' The words were uttered on a note of grudging approval.

'I'm sorry,' said Dinmont, unable to believe his ears, 'but *what* did you say?'

Sneed repeated his observation.

Dinmont felt slightly out of his depth. 'Of course I've put my socks on,' he said. 'What do you expect? I always wear socks.'

'You were not wearing socks the other day,' replied Sneed darkly.

'What on earth do you mean?' Dinmont was getting rather annoyed. 'When wasn't I wearing them?'

'Last Tuesday,' said Sneed. 'In here. I saw you.'

'But look here,' said Dinmont, 'a man can't *forget* to put on his socks.'

'I never said you forgot,' Sneed pointed out. He picked up the *Tatler* again.

'But damn it all,' cried Dinmont, nettled and bemused, 'are you suggesting that I'm the sort of chap who deliberately goes about London without any socks on?'

'I'm not suggesting anything,' Sneed replied. 'All I said was that you had put your socks on this morning. It's perfectly true. I can't see them now that you are standing up, but I could when you were sitting opposite me. Surely there's no need for you to get cross?'

At this point Dinmont, who is an equable man with a good sense of humour, realised that this insane argument might go on for ever. Muttering something about having to lunch early, he broke contact and made for the dining room.

He happened to sit next to me (this is a true story, by the way) and lost no time in telling me of his experience. He explained that it had already begun to assume a dream-like quality in his mind and that he was anxious to pass on a first-hand account to someone else before his memories of what had passed between him and Sneed dissolved or became distorted.

We agreed that to commend a man for wearing socks in his club was a subtler form of character-assassination than asking him if he had stopped beating his wife. Dinmont admitted that he felt seriously disconcerted by the allegation that he had not been wearing socks on the previous Tuesday. He knew it was not true and maintained that it could not be true, being against nature; it was, he reasoned, a physical impossibility to omit a *penultimate* process when dressing. You could put on a shirt and forget to put on a tie, but you couldn't put on a tie and forget to put on a shirt. By the same token (argued Dinmont, whose whole intellect was by now working on the problem with a feverish vigour) you couldn't, even if you were an absent-minded professor in a back number of *Punch*, stuff your bare feet into a pair of shoes without noticing that something was wrong.

I said I agreed with all this, but why had Sneed broken his customary silence to make this strange allegation?

'I only wish I knew,' muttered Dinmont, eating smoked salmon with a hunted air. 'It isn't the sort of charge that you'd think a man would fabricate, even if he had a motive for doing so. In a way that's what makes it so disturbing. I can't *prove* that I was wearing socks last Tuesday. I can't even say that I remember putting my socks on, because one does that sort of thing automatically.'

'You could appeal for witnesses,' I suggested.

'But nobody sees your socks,' said Dinmont, 'unless you happen to sit down in an armchair, which I hardly ever do. Besides, think what a fool I should look if the secretary put up a notice asking anyone who can vouch for the fact that I was wearing socks last Tuesday to get in touch with him. People would think I was going round the bend.' There was a distraught note in his voice.

'You mustn't let this get you down,' I said. 'The important thing is to watch for Sneed's next move. He's bound to show his hand sooner or later. When he does, we shall know how to act.'

Sneed has not shown his hand. For five years Dinmont and I and one or two others have kept him under observation. When opportunity offers we carry the war into the enemy's country by directing casual but pregnant glances at his socks. But our expectation that he would strike again has proved groundless. He seems to have relapsed into otherness.

Once, about two years ago, a report reached us which seemed to indicate that this front might be reactivated, that the lizard on the wall was about to abandon the *couchant regardant* for some more positive posture. Sneed, having polished off his Irish stew, was heard to order an ice.

'Certainly, sir,' said the waitress. 'What kind would you like? Chocolate?'

Sneed gave her a furious, affronted look.

'Chocolate!' he barked. '*Certainly not!*'

But when they brought him a vanilla ice he ate it up like a lamb. He remains an enigma.

6 December 1957

I've left your father for a panda.

ALAN GIBSON

HIGH LITTLETON

High Littleton, to which I have recently moved, is in that part of the county of Avon which used to be Somerset. I have now lived in all the counties of the beloved West Country. High Littleton is not the kind of village you see on the candy boxes. It was a mining place, in the middle of the North Somerset coalfield, a coalfield now dead, and indeed dying almost from the time it was born: those lumpy little hills which add such charming variety to an already beautiful landscape are mostly old slag heaps, mastered by grass for a century or so. We live, as best we can until the builders have finished the renovations, in a house which began life about three hundred years ago, as a huddle of tiny labourers' cottages (they must have been tiny labourers, because every time I stand up incautiously I bump my head). It became a pub during the mining boom, and although it must have been a small pub, it makes a substantial cottage.

When I was a young man, I held the office of Foundsman No. 1 in a beer-drinking society, based on the BBC in Bristol, though its influence spread far beyond it, called The Weaker Brethren. Frank Gillard had inadvertently christened it ('Some of the brethren are inclined to be a little weak in these matters'). The principle of the society was that when you were asked to have another pint, you weakened, and had one. Certain exceptions were allowed under the general heading of *force majeure*. A wife; a mistress, if she was pretty (but whether she was pretty or not had to be decided by the Committee of Foundsmen, and I do not remember any member putting this clause to the test); a division in the House of Commons, in the case of brother Mallalieu; a suit to plead in court, in the case of brother Kendall-Carpenter. Brother Kendall-Carpenter was allowed not to drink on Friday nights, a privilege of which he did not always avail himself. He is now headmaster of

Wellington School, Somerset, and unlike most direct-grant headmasters, has endeavoured to take his school into the comprehensive system, only to be rebuffed. The song of this society was taken from a mediaeval Latin carol, by Foundsman No. 4 (as I remember), who was also granted the title of Motto-Maker. (He is now Religious Broadcasting Organiser in Northern Ireland, which when you come to think of it is much what you would expect.) The verse began,

Meum est propositum
In taberna mori

(which may be translated, roughly, 'It is my intention to die in a pub'). Vigorously did we sing it to the tune of 'Good King Wenceslas.' So when I saw that this little house in High Littleton was called 'The Old Market Tavern', I knew that the shell had my number on it.

The village itself is long, hardly more than one busy main road, with a few housing estates hobbled on. The side roads usually tilt down to the main road, and the skateboarders do their best to kill themselves. The chairman of the parish council, who is also a builder, has offered to make a rink in the rec., for a thousand pounds, which I dare say might be a generous gesture. The High Littleton Skateboard Club is organising a jumble sale to raise the money, and the lads have been washing cars and selling firesticks to help. All this, I think, is good. It is not so much that you mind the little blighters getting killed; it is the awful thought that you might kill them. But what a waste of money High Littleton's skateboard-rink will seem in, say, five years' time, when everyone has forgotten about the stupid game, as they did the cycle speedway, and come to that the yo-yo. What shall we be left with then? A useless lump of curving concrete in the middle of our recreation ground. I expect if it saves the lives of a child or two, and the agonies of a driver or two, it is worthwhile. I promise not to write about skateboards again. My ten-year-old son has one, which adds at least thirty seconds to my evening prayers.

Now that we are sufficiently settled in to haul some of the books from their packing-cases, I was pleased to be reminded that I have about a dozen of R. A. H. Goodyear. In this paper on 10 December I read that when Benny Green was a boy, of all the books he was given at Christmas, only one provided a perfect confluence of hope and fulfilment, a volume whose title and author he had never heard of since, *The Four Schools*, by R. A. H. Goodyear. Now Mr Green is up on me in one respect. I have never read *The Four Schools*. I did not know that such a book existed. But not to have otherwise heard of Goodyear! During the year 1977 my son Adam and I, who enjoy a reading session in the evening, read six Goodyear books, much to our pleasure. We varied them occasionally (*Three Men in a Boat*, *The Wind in the Willows*) but when it was Adam's turn to choose, he went for the Goodyears. Goodyear was one of an almost extinct breed, the public school story writers. The public school story, a genre neglected by critics, did not really begin with Thomas Hughes (far too candid) and Dean Farrar (far too moral). It was Talbot Baines Reed who got it going, in the early days of the *Boys' Own Paper*. He was holy – at least he felt it necessary to make holy gestures to his publishers, the SPCK – but if anyone who has read them does not think that, for instance, *The Fifth Form at St Dominic's*, or *The Master of the Shell* are not good books, then the man is an ass.

After Reed came Frank Richards, who wrote for working-class boys, wrote in enormous quantities, survived to make George Orwell apologise for thinking he was a syndicate: I wonder if any man has ever had more words printed? There were much more solemn books, not all of them bad, written by people with names like Gunby Hadath and Hylton Cleaver. And there was Goodyear, muddling along in between, never quite sure which sort to be, but writing about two books a year for twenty years – probably more. I wonder who he was. A northerner, certainly. A soccer man (he makes a Robert of himself when he tries to write about rugby). Probably a schoolmaster at some stage of his life. I would be interested to hear from anyone who knew him. In the meantime, I promise, next time I go to London, to take to Benny Green – only lending – *The Captain and the Kings*, which is one of the best school stories I have ever read.

I have wandered some way from High Littleton, and I have not got round to saying a word about the Lib-Lab pact (like every other Liberal, I hold deep feelings about it, but am not quite sure what they are); and I meant to tell you about *The Times*, a paper I love and strive to serve, which has just issued a crushing memorandum on the use of the word 'gambit' (if the memorandum is right, the Shorter Oxford is wrong, to say nothing of Stephen Potter); but I have not left myself space. I sit here at High Littleton, and if there was a moon I could see Glastonbury Tor on the horizon. *Meum est propositum in taberna mori.* My cat Crumbs, the only cat the names of whose kittens were balloted for by *Times* readers, sits comfortably at my feet. She wishes a Happy New Year to all her readers, and reports well of country life.

14 January 1978

ANDREW GIMSON

SUN AND SEX

When I told Mr David Bird I was going on a Club 18–30 holiday, he implored me to reconsider. 'They'll tear you to shreds,' he said. 'You've got to be street-wise to go on one of those. When you talk they'll think you're taking the piss.'

Mr Bird is a compositor at Saffron Graphics, where the *Spectator*'s pages are typeset, and the workers are prone to levity. 'He'll lose his virginity out there,' one of the younger printers predicted.

Mr Bruce Anderson, of the *Sunday Telegraph*, demanded that on my return I give my score. A colleague in Doughty Street told me about an acquaintance of hers called Jaqqi, a waitress from Leeds. Jaqqi was well pleased by her Club 18–30 holiday. She had 'seven lads in 14 days', but her most exciting experience was to be covered in crisps, which the men had to eat off her.

The club 18–30 brochure explained how I was feeling:

THE TIME OF YOUR LIFE IS HERE

The time is now. You're young, independent and looking for excitement. You know what you want, and you want to get it before it's too late. You want to see and be seen. You are the scene.

You're not alone. All over the country there are people like you making the most of their freedom, determined to live life to the limit before they get trapped within the system. They too want to get away from their everyday surroundings, to spend their hard-earned holidays not stuck in some boring British seaside town watching the rain, but basking on a sun-kissed beach, sharing the days and nights with new friends who speak their language. . . .

The brochure was full of pictures of beautiful girls and handsome men, on beaches kissed by the sun. After long thought I decided to go to Majorca, which with Ibiza and Corfu is one of Club 18–20's most popular destinations.

'You can leave that "good book" for another holiday if you're coming to Majorca,' the brochure told me. It said I should book accommodation which was exclusive to Club 18–30: 'you can be sure that there will be no old fogeys complaining about the noise, and no screaming kids to disturb you. It also means the party never stops.'

I chose an exclusive hotel in Arenal, about seven miles south-east of Palma. A week's stay cost £147.95, including flights to and from Gatwick, a single room (£19.25 more than sharing), breakfast and insurance. There was some criticism at the *Spectator* of my decision to incur the extra expense of a single room, but I tried to suggest it would enable me to seduce an even larger number of girls.

I landed at Palma airport one morning in early May. An attractive girl from Newcastle upon Tyne was standing on the far side of the customs post, which I went quickly through, having only cabin baggage. She was the Club 18–30 Rep. She told me there were eight other arrivals on my flight, of whom six were girls.

One by one, after long delay, my fellow passengers emerged from customs. They carried enormous suitcases. It would be unkind to mention the various disfigurements from which they suffered. None resembled the people in the brochure more closely than I did myself. I started to fear that its pictures had shown the Platonic essence of the Club 18–30 girl, laid up in heaven.

We left for our hotels in taxis. I found myself alone in a taxi with the Rep. She had spotted my rapaciousness and sat in front with the driver.

Arenal is a dump. Most of it has been shoddily built in the last 20 years. The hotel where I stayed is shoddier than many. I left my luggage in my room, which enjoyed a good view of the sea, and went to explore. The Rep attached to my hotel, a friendly young man from Stevenage, said he would meet me later with some of the people who were arriving on other flights, in order to describe the many 'goodtimes' arranged for us.

Walking round Arenal I found that it contains, among other pubs, the Henry VIII, Victoria, Lord Nelson, Red Lion, Welsh Dragon, Auld Boozer, Pink Panther, Rover's Return, Faulty [*sic*] Towers, EastEnders and Coach and Horses. I went into the Coach and Horses. The interior is half-timbered and decorated with pictures of coaching scenes. The governor, Stan, used to have a pub in South Shields. He has not seen a fight in seven years in Arenal and does not throw people out. He said, however, that the 18–30s were 'animals'.

When I returned to the hotel, I seated myself near a man who was describing the 11 murders which have taken place in the Slough area this year. He had witnessed only one.

'Where you from?'

'London.'

'Don't sound like it.'

'Only since 1979.'

'I'd've thought you'd've picked a bit up.'

Later on, someone told me I didn't have an accent. Nobody seemed to think I was taking the piss. Poor old Bird, I thought, wrong again.

We drank beer. Drinking was the most uninterrupted theme of the holiday. I was told a story about a man who was sick and started to eat it. Among the Club 18–30 notices in the hotel was one informing us: 'Drunk people will not be allowed on the plane.' The man from Slough told me how much his tattoos cost. Many of the men were tattooed.

At seven o'clock, three drunks entered singing a football chant. They danced on a table, to the irritation of the barman. I met a Marine called Yorkie, who was afterwards to try to help me.

That night, we went to a sunglasses party in another hotel, organised by the Reps. 'Those without sunglasses will be stripped naked,' I was told. The Reps moved among us, encouraging us to have fun. We were determined to have fun whether they encouraged us or not, but in order to leave nothing to chance they organised team games. In one of these one had the opportunity, each time the music stopped, to adopt a 'Latin lover' position with one's partner. There was also a competition between five of the men, to see which could most quickly eat a plate of crisps and two bits of garlic bread, drink a bottle of beer and a glass of peppermint liqueur and smoke a cigarette. Later I went to the Piccadilly Corner, a popular pub and disco, and to another disco called Snoopy's. Much later, I returned to the hotel. Throughout the night it resounded to shrieks and chants as if it were a madhouse, though I suppose the inmates of modern madhouses are drugged not to shriek.

My memory of the next six days is blurred. The scenes which follow are based on notes in my diary. Some of these are too disjointed to mean anything even to me. Phrases such as 'Played 20: won none' defy interpretation.

But a few images remain in focus. Many of the girls were pretty. I was especially charmed by a girl from the West Country, who not only looked but sounded delightful. We fell into conversation, and I so quickly heard her story, or part of it, that I realised it could not be especially private.

She had a boyfriend at home. This sounded a standard Bunburying gambit: many of the girls had boyfriends at home, fidelity to whom could be made to seem as noble as Algernon's concern for Bunbury. There was, on the other hand, a more encouraging way of pointing out where the boyfriend was.

Her boyfriend was looking after their seven-month-old baby. He was unemployed so she was working. He thought she was somewhere else in England. She had just had a miscarriage. She didn't want to get married because she didn't love the boyfriend enough. She had had to come on holiday because it was all getting too much for her.

'Why are you looking at me like that?' she asked, in her beautiful West Country accent. 'I'm sorry to be rude but it embarrasses me.'

My pathetic excuse, that I was thinking she was the sort of girl a latter-day Thomas Hardy might write a novel about, did not work. The name Hardy meant nothing to her.

The Reps offered us a programme of 'goodtimes' during the week at an extra cost of £79. I went on three of these, costing about £45, on the grounds that this was the price given in the brochure. One was a beach party attended by 320 18–30s and 18 Reps. Another was a barbecue. A third was a show called 'The Pirates Adventure', attended by about 400 of us.

In the coach on our way to the Pirates, I sat next to Yorkie. It appeared to him that I was having less than his success with the girls. He offered me some of his chat-up lines. For example, he would take an overflowing ashtray up to a girl he fancied and say to her: 'This exquisite antique could be yours if you become my lover.'

'Does it work?'

'One in ten,' he said. 'The girl in the red dress is after your parts.'

'How do you know?'

'I can tell.'

When we reached the Pirates we found ourselves sitting nowhere near Red Dress, but next to two girls called Loraine and Tracy. We had dinner, diverted by an excellent pantomime. The Pirates were also acrobats. There was unlimited wine to drink.

After the panto, I asked Loraine to dance. She said Tracy would like to dance with me. Many of the girls had arrived with a girlfriend, who could be used, or not, as a means of protection even more reliable than an absent boyfriend. I did not want to dance with Tracy, so went in search of Red Dress. Red Dress gave me a regretful look over the shoulder of the man around whom she was already fastened.

I returned to Yorkie, 'I don't think Red Dress is that attractive,' I said.

'You stupid bugger leaving it until half-way through the evening.'

At five to 12, just before our coach was due to leave, I went outside. Several people were being sick. One girl looked as though she might choke. Two Reps came up, took hold of her in a practised way and ordered her to be properly sick.

When we got on the coach, we were warned that we would be fined '1,000 pesetas a throw' if we vomited. The Reps organised a singsong on the way back to Arenal. Several people were sick into bags. As we drove past Palma's magnificent cathedral, floodlit above us, we were singing a song of which the sense, if not the exact wording, was 'Sex is good for you'.

The cathedral was built by the Christian invaders of Majorca. One day, in direct contravention of orders, I caught a bus from Arenal to Palma and went to see it. The whole of old Palma is worth seeing and the cathedral crowns the town. Two of its features immediately catch the visitor's eye: the serried buttresses of the southern façade, and the extraordinarily high nave. Its columns are, according to the guidebook, nearly twice as high as those of Chartres, but only half as thick. This guide says of Majorca:

> For the enchasing [sic] beauty of its shores, its flowering vegetation, for the caressing sun and benign climate, it has come to be called 'The paradise Isle'. It is not strange, therefore, that through the centuries so much beauty has been much coveted, and for this reason the island was seized by the plundering Moorish ships; the Moors having long wished for so precious a pearl. The island was under Moslem rule for more than three centuries.
>
> The year 1229 was the year of its 'Liberation', of its 'Conquest'. King Jaime I, a vigorous man of strong character, with a fleet of 170 large ships . . . sailed from . . . the Catalonian coast. . . . The story runs that, as the ships approached on the night of 7 September in the year 1229, there broke loose a tempest so violent that the expedition seemed doomed to failure; wherupon the King, praying for guidance, on the poop of his ship *Montpeller*, made a vow to erect a church under the advocation of our Lady St Mary, Mother of God.

I am afraid the pagan invaders of Majorca who arrived in their millions in the latter half of the 20th century did not build anything so fine. The Christian invaders destroyed the Arab monuments they found, but the pagans ignored the Christian monuments. Instead they destroyed the coast, especially where it was sandy.

Descending to the sea to gain a better view of the cathedral and the palace next to it, I found a notice stencilled in black paint onto a concrete pillar:

MAJORQUINS
YOU ARE SHIT
U.S. NAVY

Beneath, in red letters, someone had sprayed:

MARINES
=HARLOTTS

It was impossible to be certain which notice had been painted first.

On my other unauthorised excursion, I walked into the country behind Arenal. It was the only time during my stay that I was reminded how wonderful the Mediterranean countryside smells, when it has not sunk under chip pans. But walkers should be warned that a major road has been built behind Arenal, and that several others are in the process of construction, as well as a gigantic leisure centre.

I asked the manager of my hotel whether he liked what the English and German visitors were doing to his island. 'The people born in Majorca, we get the money to live very well,' he said. 'With the young ones, maybe they make some trouble when they drink too much, but generally they are not bad people. It's very nice work. I love it. You know many people during the summer, you get friends with these people, most of them say thank you very much, we've had a nice holiday. I hope we get tourists for 100 years. I think the English people are not as the news on the television shows, because I work with the English for 20 years. There were more gentlemen before than now. But I don't want to mean they're very bad now. The Germans are good but the English are as good as the Germans. When you are drunk, you cannot have control of yourself, whatever nationality you are.' However much I pressed him, he maintained, and evidently believes, that the tourists and the money they bring are a blessing to Majorca.

On the last day I wore my Michael Heath tee-shirt, which bears a drawing by Heath of a yob wearing a tee-shirt, on which are the words 'ANOTHER IDIOT WITH WRITING ON HIS TEE-SHIRT'. Under that are the words 'The Spectator', but nobody attached much significance to them. I was hoping that the garment might especially appeal when I went to the disco, but first I met a man to whom I had talked in the Welsh Dragon the night before. He had been in the Army. 'What did you do afterwards?' I had asked. 'Went to prison,' he had replied, with a look which discouraged further inquiry. 'Domestic trouble.'

Now we went for a drink, and I heard about his lifelong

hatred of authority. Another court appearance hangs over him, so I do not want to write much at the moment. It was, however, the first time I had talked to anyone who has a passionate loathing of the police. To a bourgeois who has never, for example, been conscripted into the army, such conversations are enlightening.

Human flesh defies the laws of cookery: lightly fried in a little oil it turns brown but fried for longer it goes pink. My own flesh remained whitish, since I flouted convention and did not fry myself. Perhaps that is why the girls laughed at me as well as my tee-shirt, or perhaps Bird was right after all about my accent. Yorkie was in despair. He was, I think, trying to save my pride when he asked, 'Have you already met the girl of your dreams?'

'Yes,' I said. Whether or not this was true, it made the situation less embarrassing for Yorkie as well as me. I recalled the advice given by the editors of *China Youth News* to a lovelorn young man jilted by his girlfriend:

To die over an unhappy love affair is absolutely worthless. You should plunge yourself into the hot struggle for production and gradually your wounds will be healed.

Production? I recalled the firm instructions the editor of the *Spectator* had given me, to enter into all the activities of people who go on Club 18–30 holidays, and asked an exquisite blonde to dance. She agreed. If only there were more space in this newspaper, I would tell you what happened next.

13 June 1987

COLIN HAYCRAFT

ARS POETICA

A new Professor of Poetry at Oxford is being elected by Convocation. The candidates are said to include Francis Warner (for the second time), E. J. Thribb, Pam Ayres, Peter Levi and John Sparrow.

Carmina quae bona sint, quae pessima, cernere paucis
contingit: nullas norunt plerique Camenas
grammaticasque tribus inhiant et pulpita[1] lippi.
ecce iterum *Monitor*, si quid monitoris eges tu,[2]
vocibus impavidus qualis stridentibus anser
urbem olim monuit: nempe ipse poemata pangit[3]
ac versu tragico vilem certavit ob hircum.[4]
circumeunt alii: garrit[5] qui ridiculus[6] *Thrips*
sermoni propiora[7] (putas hunc esse poetam[8]
cui per humum repit[9] sua musa pedestris?)[10] et illa
quae, dum vitat humum, nubes et inania captat,[11]
et cui deficiunt sectanti *levia* nervi,[12]
quemque puella fovet pullum lasciva Catulli.
serpit humi tumidus[13] *Thrips, Passer* pipilat, anser
clamat, nec sane *leviter* flant *Aëres* isti,
tanto cum strepitu[14] genus irritabile vatum[15]
rixatur. quando haec ecludet iurgia finis?[16]
grammatici certant et adhuc sub iudice lis est.[17]

[1]Horace, *Ep.*1.19.40 [2]*Ep.*1.18.67 [3]*Ep.*1.18.40 [4]*AP*220 [5]*Sat.*1.10.41 [6]*AP* 139 [7]*Sat.*1.4.42 [8]Ibid. [9]*Ep.*2.1.251 [10]*Sat.*2.6.17 [11]*AP* 230 [12]*AP* 26 [13]*AP* 28 (timidus *codd.*) [14]*Ep.*2.1.203 [15]*Ep.*2.2.102 [16]*Ep.*2.1.38 [17]*AP* 78

The following is a translation of the Latin:

Few people have the good fortune to be able tell good poetry from bad: most have no knowledge of the Muses and gape, bleary-eyed, at the tribes of professors at their lecture-stands.

Now here comes Warner to advise you (supposing you need advice), with strident clamour like the intrepid goose which once warned the city: he, of course, writes poetry himself and has contended with tragic verse for a cheap goat [i.e. has written plays]. Others too are doing the rounds: the absurd Thribb [*thrips* = a worm] who babbles in verse which is more like prose (do you regard him, whose pedestrian muse crawls along the ground, as a *poet*?); she who avoids the ground but catches at clouds and inanities instead; he who aims at smoothness (*levia*) but fails in inspiration; and the chick whom Catullus's lascivious girl cherished [i.e. Lesbia's sparrow].

The tumid worm creeps along the earth, the sparrow chirps, the goose cries, the airs blow far from softly (*leviter*) – so noisily does the irritable race of poets fight. When will there be an end to these quarrels? The professors strive. The case is not yet decided.

4 November 1978

I was expecting a wolf.

RICHARD INGRAMS

RECYCLED TELEVISION

Returning home after a few days in sleepy Ireland I am struck, as always, by the facts (a) that I have missed nothing while I have been away and (b) that there is nothing of any merit waiting to be watched now that I am back. I thought this year the schedules for Bank Holiday Monday reached a new low. There wasn't a single programme on offer that a person of even below average intelligence would want to watch let alone anything that a discerning critic could write about in what Kingsley Amis has generously described as 'a fairly entertaining magazine'. There seemed nothing for it but to get outside and make preparations for the winter that will soon be with us.

One of my greatest pleasures in recent weeks has been operating a device called a Briketpresse which converts old newspapers into combustible blocks. All you do is soak your old *Daily Telegraph*s, or *Spectator*s in a plastic dustbin overnight and then compress the black squishy pulp into the Bricketpresse, squeeze the water out and hey presto you have a neat rectangular brick about the size of an Irish block of peat which after a few days drying in the sun is ready to burn.

I had been waiting for the onset of autumn before saying anything in public about my new cottage industry, until, that is, I had seen whether they actually did burn as the manufacturers said they would. I can now report that I have seen the future and it works. The bricks do not as you might expect burst into flames, they simmer quietly away rather like peat, giving off a fair amount of heat. Whether it amounts to 4,150 Kcal/kg, as the manufacturers claim, I am not enough of a scientist to say.

The satisfaction you get out of this activity has nothing really to do with economics, although there is an obvious financial advantage when coal costs about £90 a ton, in getting a supply of fuel for nothing. The real pleasure comes from putting news-

*"Many of you will find the following programme
deeply offensive and shocking . . . ."*

papers – trashy, dirty, overpriced things – to a useful purpose.
Until you have done it, you have no idea what fun it is to
crumple up a copy of Lord Matthews's *Daily Express*, plunge it
into water with a fork and reduce it to pulp in the knowledge
that the following day it will be on its way to becoming an
economical fuel.

I just keep wishing that there was some similar way in which
television programmes could be recycled and put to good use.
The nearest I can get to it is ripping up a copy of the *Radio
Times* and soaking it; though you have to be careful here as the
shiny advertising pages will not disintegrate in the water and
have to be disposed of separately. Then there is all the publicity
bumf that the BBC puts out which breaks up quite well, and
which printed wastefully on one side only also makes quite
good notepaper (in fact this article was originally drafted on it).

But there is really no beneficial side-effect that you can derive
from your television set that would be like the newspaper
bricks. The best thing you can do is to get rid of it altogether. If
you have a colour television set this would mean an annual
saving of £50, more than enough to invest in a Briketpresse

which comes at the slightly exorbitant price of £32.38 (inc VAT).

4 September 1982

GOING OFF?

I see that we continue to be exercised here at the *Spectator* by the mystery of Rees-Mogg and *Dallas*. Auberon Waugh and myself are both sceptical about his claim on a recent *Panorama* that *Dallas* is his favourite programme along with *Dr Who*. Mr Waugh advances the theory that in saying this Mogg may have been trying to endear himself to members of the Workers' Collective at the *Times*. I doubt if this is so. The so-called Workers' Collective is, as far as I can gather, composed of Mr Rees-Mogg's equals, men of the calibre of Charles Douglas-Home and the paper's brilliant legal correspondent, Marcel Berlins. It would have been more plausible to argue that Rees-Mogg was trying to suck up to the print unions, whose co-operation in any new system is not yet assured. But then, one asks, why drag in *Dr Who*? Rees-Mogg may be the teeniest bit out of touch with contemporary trends but he surely cannot think prosperous SOGAT and NATSOPA members spend their leisure hours watching Tom Baker do his stuff? Personally I think the reference to *Dr Who* contains the clue to the great *Dallas*-Rees-Mogg riddle. Rees-Mogg is not trying to suck up to his colleagues or to the print workers; he is trying to suck up to his children. At least I hope he is.

To those of us who like to think that in spite of everything that has happened to Britain people remain a fund of toleration and good sense, one of the most disconcerting pieces of evidence to the contrary is provided weekly in the list of the top ten television programmes. This used to show, I think, that the Neanderthal Bruce Forsyth and his *Generation Game* was far more popular than anything else. Now it is the turn of the degrading soap opera *Dallas*. Here, surely, says Mr Waugh, is cause for despair, and I am tempted to agree at first sight. But supposing what I half suspect to be the case is true, that the bulk of TV viewers consists of children, then the high score for Forsyth and *Dallas* makes sense. In fact Mr Waugh in his learned exegesis admits that in his own case it is his children who are responsible for his having to degrade himself by watching the programme. In heartrending tones he writes how 'in the reduced circumstances of the times, we now have only one room heated and *there was no question of trying to prevent my children from watching it*' (my italics). Mr Waugh goes on to bemoan general collapse but all it amounts to, perhaps, is that certain fathers – for example Waugh, Rees-Mogg and, I have to admit, myself – are not taking a firm enough line. In my case this may not matter so much. But how can Rees-Mogg hope to stand up to SOGAT if he dare not switch off his TV set when he feels like it?

I know from experience that there is a tendency to say after a suitable interval that such and such a programme, hailed not so long before as being the height of fashion, has now 'gone off'. It happened to the Muppets, long since deserted by the Trendies but still – as the inspired programme on Sunday proved – as good as ever. On the other hand, having watched it reasonably faithfully during its new series I do think that *Not the Nine O'Clock News* has 'gone off'. For the first time this week I think I sat through the whole programme with nary a titter. One of the admirable things about the programme was always that none of its sketches lasted longer than about two minutes, so that if any one was below par, it was soon over. Recently however some sketches have been allowed to drag on in a way that recalled the longeurs of late period Sherrin. Only a wonderful *Nationwide* a week or so ago has been up to scratch. The *Not the Nine O'Clock News* team are now under exactly the same pressures as *That Was The Week*. They are famous. They are doing books and records. They are being made tempting offers no doubt by a variety of tycoons. Given what has happened to groups like this in the past the likelihood is that they may soon split up. In other cases this wouldn't matter but it would be a great pity if we were to lose a team which has shown so great a talent for exposing the absurdity of television. If the future generation is being brought up on a diet of tat like *Dallas* they ought also to see something that tells them what rubbish it all is.

6 December 1980

JASPISTOS

THE READERS' COMPETITIONS

Jaspistos reports: Competitors were asked for an embarrassing letter, accompanying a literary offering, from a hopeful author to publisher.

The rather large (!!) parcel that comes with this letter is my thought poem, *My Friends the Trees*. I know you will be interested in it because you are a Sagittarius. It is written on a special paper made from rabbits' doings that is my own invention because trees do not like to be made into paper but rabbit doings do not mind. I know this because the trees told me. My poem, which is my own story, tells more what the trees said to me and I have made it so each different coloured ink SIGNIFIES a different sort of tree; for instance, orange is an orange tree. All but the last 1,000 pages I did in SECRET WRITING so CERTAIN PEOPLE could not read it. Please send the money in postal orders or THEY will steal it. I must warn you BAD LUCK COMES TO HIM who disobeys the trees.

(Balthazar Ngaga)
1 March 1980

Jaspistos reports: Competitors were asked to boil down barbarously some well-known poem.

> *A Valediction Forbidding Mourning*
> I'm off; but cool it: after all
> the separation's physical.
> Twixt minds, though distant,
>   there's a link:
> we may not —— , but we can
>   think.
>
> (M. Mortimer)

The Wreck of the 'Deutschland'
Five nuns
Exiled by Huns
Lost, drowned;
God-found!
(Tony Brode)

The Lady of Shalott
Saw knight pass
In glass,
Left room,
Full of gloom,
Stole boat,
Died afloat.
(Fiona Pitt-Kethley)

Lycidas
College mate
Lost at sea;
Could same fate
Lurk for me?
Would have been
Perfect pastor;
Present scene
Sheer disaster.
Don't cry; he's OK
Got my coat; on my way.
(O. Smith)

The Ancient Mariner
Old salt
Grabs third,
Tells what
Once occurred.
His fault:
'Shot bird,
Saw ghost,
Crew die,
Ship lost,
Not I.'
(John Sweetman)

The Solitary Reaper
Up hill creeping
Saw her reaping,
Singing, bending,
Song heart-rending.
What? Cannot say;
But lovely lay!

(P. W. R. Foot)

The Listeners
'Who's at home?' Traveller
    knocks.
Bangs again. Violent shocks
Wake the ghosts. Phantom
    hosts
Hear the din. No one in.
Final whack. Calls 'I'm back.
Had to try.' No reply.
Gallops down lanes.
Silence reigns.

(Jean Hayes)

Mariana
In ancient nook,
Midst dreary ground –
He's slung his hook,
I hang around.

(Jill Hingyi)

Dover Beach
Sitting on the brink,
Staring at the drink,
Makes a fellow think.
Thinking leads to doubt,
If you don't watch out
(There's a lot of it about).
And if you don't take care,
Doubt leads to despair . . .
Oh, isn't life unfair?

(N. C. Andrews)

Horatius
Tuscans manic –
Romans panic;
Bold Horatius –
Plan sagacious;
Bridge is held
By three while felled;
Foes expunged –
Hero plunged.
Cheers and glory –
Grandsires' story.
                    (Mary Holtby)
                    9 October 1982

Jaspistos reports: Competitors were asked to describe the features of a very ill-run hotel or boarding-house which a guest should prepare himself for.

The taxi-man has never heard of it.
Meals have to be paid for in advance.
The wine waiter recommends the Wincarnis.
The chef lunches at the pub down the road.
The dressing-table drawers are lined with copies of the *News Chronicle*.
The notice advertising Vacancies is screwed to the front gate.
                    (Pat Blackford)

There is an animated knot of guests around the visitors' book, puzzling over something original to write in the Comments column.
The Gideon Bibles are well-thumbed.
Every room boasts an original Tretchikoff.

99

"I still feel hungry".

The fire extinguisher is scorched.
There is a collecting box in the front entrance for donations to
the Great Ormond Street Hospital for Sick Children.
There is a pets' section on the menu.

(Nell L. Wregible)

The owner is a former sociology lecturer, but this is 'more
creative and independent'.
The teenage son cooks, very slowly.
Breakfast starts after the first Monday morning train to
London.

(C. Brownlie)

Psychos in the showers.
Creatures in the crudités.
More salmonella than salmon in the mousse.

(O. Banfield)

Any guest arriving with luggage is viewed with suspicion.

(J. Beales)

Certain lounge chairs are reserved for certain residents.

(A. C. Hannay)
19 February 1983

Jaspistos reports: Competitors were asked for a description of conduct unbecoming to either a lady or a gentleman.

Certain things one just doesn't do, does one? *A*ssassinate spiders in baths. *B*reak wind in the company of archbishops. *C*opulate in Royal Parks. *D*rink Corsican sherry. *E*at faggots without mushy peas. *F*asten seat-belts in dodgems. *G*o to Benidorm. *H*eckle Screaming Lord Sutch. *I*nquire whether potential bed-mates have herpes. *J*uggle with plovers' eggs. *K*arate-chop neighbours' cats. *L*ie unprofitably. *M*uddle Monet and Manet. *N*obble the Jockey Club. *O*pen Income Tax demands. *P*ee in hosts' wash-basins. *Q*uestion God. *R*ead the *TV Times*. *S*iphon off OAPs' petrol. *T*out VALA membership. *U*nderstand monetarism. *V*ideo-record Russell Harty. *W*ear jodhpurs in bed. *X*erox the Book of Revelation. *Y*odel in taxis. *Z*ig-zag down the M6.

(Andrew McEvoy)

Belonging to the Order of Buffaloes in Everton and putting OBE after your name.
  Including more than one foreign coin in contributions to the church collection.
  When being treated at the VD clinic, naming as contacts those who spurned your advances.

(George Moor)

Completing the crossword in your host's newspaper before he has seen it.

Heightening, by pretended stupefaction, the embarrassment of someone who has by a word revealed unremarkable ignorance.

Peering round the shoulder of the person at the head of the bank queue and closely observing the transaction.

Standing with hand in trouser pocket during Evensong, rattling keys and raising and lowering heels to an unheard, inner drumbeat.

(Paul Wigmore)

Saying 'Good evening t' you' or, worse, 'A *very* good evening t' you'.

Referring to parents by their christian names.

Providing a choice of toilet paper.

(J. H. M. Donald)

Lighting a pipe while proposing marriage.

Drawing a faint line to mark the whisky bottle level.

Talking about computers in mixed company.

(Gerry Hamill)

Testing the temperature of a drink with your finger.

Drawing attention to the pattern on your pyjamas.

Spitting on a journalist without first being spat upon.

(Llewellin Berg)

Capping or improving another person's joke, however mangled in the telling.

Admitting to loving one's wife.

(Gerald Benson)

Belonging to Mensa.

(D. B . Jenkinson)

Upsetting your glass and appropriating your host's while he mops up.

(C.P.F.)
7 April 1984

Charles Seaton reports: On the pattern of

Full fathom five thy father lies:
His aqualung was the wrong size

competitors were asked to 'improve' well-known single lines or
couplets in a like spirit of fun.

My true love hath my heart and I have his;
What clever stuff this transplant business is!

There was a sound of revelry by night;
The Commons, sitting late, sat also tight.

(Patricia Stockbridge)

Orpheus with his lute made trees
Subject to Dutch Elm Disease.

(Paul Griffin)

It is a beauteous evening, calm and free;
Why did you have to mention pregnancy?

(Poppy Pratt)

No coward soul is mine,
But please – not parsnip wine.

(Noel Petty)

When lovely woman stoops to folly
With royal Andrew – gosh, the lolly!

(Martin Fagg)

Lives of great men all remind us
We can make our lives sublime,
But, regrettably, you'll find us
Watching telly half the time.

(Peter Hadley)

I leant upon a coppice gate
And found it could not bear my weight.

(Joyce Johnson)

Ethereal minstrel! Pilgrim of the sky!
Why must you spatter all the passers-by?

(Fiona Pitt-Kethley)

I will arise and go now, and go to Innisfree,
It's the only place in Ireland for a decent cup of tea.

(Nicholas Hodgson)

If I should die, think only this of me:
He never made it to Gallipoli.

(Roy Dean)

Come into the garden, Maud
– I can promise you won't be bored.

(John Sweetman)

The Harlot's Cry from Street to Street
Shall weave Old England's winding Sheet,
But worse for England's Weal than that
Is Scargill in his silly Hat.

(W. F. N. Watson)

And the long labours of the toilet cease,
For Ex-Lax offers you a quick release.

Full nakedness! All joys are due to thee –
AIDS, sunburn, insect bites, to name but three.

(I. D. M. Morley)

Beautiful Eveyln Hope is dead
– She drove straight on when the lights were red.

(O. Smith)

Miss Joan Hunter Dunn, Miss Joan Hunter Dunn,
Take off your knickers and let's have some fun.

(Basil Ransome-Davies)

When you are old and gray and full of sleep
You do not need to bother counting sheep.

(D. A. Prince)

My Mistress' eyes are nothing like the sun,
More like two currants in a penny bun.

(Ginger Jones)

Go, for they call you, shepherd, from the hill;
Another darned hang-glider's had a spill.

(George Moor)

Tell me not here, it needs not saying
That you'll have lobster if I'm paying.

(J. C. M. Hepple)

Busy old fool, unruly Sun,
Just suppose the Argies won.

(J. C. Causer)

They told me, Heraclitus, they told me you were dead,
But I just wondered who you were and what on earth you'd
    said.

(Guy Hankin)

A sweet disorder in the dress
Suggests a bedroom in a mess.

(Llewellin Berg)

Under the greenwood tree
Is seldom earwig-free.

(Mary Holtby)

Beneath those rugged elms, that yew-tree's shade,
On that flat tombstone grandmama was laid.

(Ralph Sadler)

'Try not the Pass!' the old man said;
'But bid a couple of Hearts instead.'

(Miss F. J. Tarrant)

(The poets drawn upon are, in order: Sidney, Byron, Shakespeare, Wordsworth, Emily Brontë, Goldsmith, Longfellow, Hardy, Wordsworth, Yeats, Rupert Brooke, Tennyson, Blake, Pope, Donne, Browning, Betjeman, Yeats, Shakespeare, Arnold, Housman, Donne, Cory, Herrick, Shakespeare, Gray, Longfellow.)

14 July 1984

He's terribly famous. He's with the secret service.

Jaspistos reports: Competitors were invited to supply amusing examples of meanness, real or invented.

But does he touch the poppy up with red ink every fifth year like the woman *I* know? She keeps a special tin of stale cake for workmen and makes their tea with re-cycled tea-bags; donates all her old *Radio Times* to the local hospital; sent her godchild a Gideon bible (wrapped in cling-film); cuts After Eights into as many quarters as there are guests; 'Buys British' . . . but only when the sherry runs out (i.e., not often); and has just reminded me that I owe her two aspirins.

(D. B . Jenkinson)

Your hostess awakes you with a cup of horrible tea and toast done on one side only; later you find tea-bags hanging up to dry in the kitchen. The bath-water is tepid and the soap consists of the congealed residues of six other brands; two harsh hand-towels await your freezing body. The luncheon rosé is composed of last night's red and white, thus prolonging a headache which the single proffered aspirin has failed to cure.

(P. Kennealy)

Saving old calendars till the right combination of days of the week and dates comes round again.

When travelling by bus always ask, 'Eez thees right for Ponderz End?' You will be put off at the next stop, but you will have made some progress towards your destination.

(Charles Mosley)

Bending down to retrieve a dropped halfpenny.

(Peter Norman)

Spelling 'meanness' with one 'n'.

Pretending to be mean when you're not.

(John O'Byrne)

Dragging the family round every bureau de change in Deauville to find the best exchange rate.
    Sending a bundle of Christmas cards to one of a group of faraway friends, for delivery by hand.
    Taking change out of the collection plate.

(Noel Petty)

Removing free gifts from comics and giving them to children as presents.
    Tippexing old Christmas cards and re-using them.

(Michael Birt)

A man I know, on hearing the Remembrance Day poppy story, could 'honestly see nothing mean in it'.

(T. Griffiths)

A man I knew wouldn't let his wife buy dishcloths. She was told to use his old underpants instead. He never washed up.

(Jean Hayes)

A wealthy traveller on our cruise bargained long with an Arab quayside trader for a carpet, finally paying him with Monopoly money.

(Ralph Sadler)
8 December 1984

You were asked for clerihews about living people.

Lord Denning, MR,
Said to a young man at the
    Bar,
'The law has all been decided.
Who decided it? I did.'
                        (David Cairns)

Ted Hughes
Wasn't much of a hand at
   clerihews.
His besetting sin
Was that cheerlessness was
   always breaking in.
(Coco)

Bob Geldof
Held off
Famine in Ethiopia
With a Pop-cornucopia.
(Jermyn Thynne)

The Bishop of Durham
Is a meeserable worrum.
On him who turns the Kirk
   arsy-vairsy
The Lord hae mercy!
(Moyra Blyth)

Anthony Wedgwood Benn
Has been making a speech
   again.
The melancholy fact is
That he is addicted to this
   practice.
(Arthur Oliver)

Charlotte Cornwell
Has shown stars who've not
   worn well
How to make big sums
Out of 'big bums'.
(Keith Norman)

If lasting fame is
The dream of Kingsley Amis,
He should try for the Booker
   Prize with a novel
About   structuralist   social

workers committing incest
in a hovel.
                              (Philip Skelsey)

Alec Douglas-Home
Was never known to fume.
Told of a missile on the way,
He'd say, 'I say!'
                              (John Crown)

Ian Paisley
Is aisley
The number one Prod
Next to God.
                       ' (Watson Weeks)

Louis Blom-Cooper
Exclaimed, 'Super!
This inquiry in Brent
Is money (on me) well spent.'
                          (Nicholas Murray)

John Paul the Second
Is generally reckoned
To spend more time in the air
Than in Peter's Chair.
                              (A. J. Ryder)

P. J. Kavanagh
Often thinks, 'I havanagh
Clue what to say.'
But it usually turns out OK.
                                (I. C. Snell)

Joanna Lumley
Is distinctly comely;
But you need to be more than
a looker
To judge the Booker.
                              (Peter Lyon)

Lord Dacre
Was deceived by a faker.
He'd never have got such a
    no-hoper
Past Hugh Trevor-Roper.
                    (Noel Petty)

Mrs Mary Whitehouse,
When taken to a lighthouse,
Was seen to gape
In horror at its phallic shape.
                    (Roy Dean)

A. J. Ayer
Finds no meaning in prayer,
Seeing no purpose served
Where   no   outcome's
    observed.
                    (P. E. Roe)

It's many years since John
    Osborne
Was born.
He's not so young any more,
But he's even angrier than
    before.
                    (Gerard Benson)

Sir Keith Joseph
Said, 'Heaven knows, if
I don't succeed with the
    teacher shakedown,
I shall have what has threat-
    ened me for years, a
    nervous breakdown.'
                    (N. E. Soret)

Roger Scruton,
Though hailed as a brute on
The political Left, is margin-
    ally pinker

Than the average Surrey
Sunday-golfing gin-drinker.
(D. A. Prince)

Lord Hartwell (we laugh)
Failed to keep the *Telegraph*
Out of the red.
Now Black's got it instead.
(John Sweetman)
18 January 1986

*"In the book club I belong to you not only get the
book you get the author too".*

P. J. KAVANAGH

ALTOGETHER NEARLY

'Excuse me, is this the Public?' The man was angled forward, weight on front foot like M. Hulot.

'No,' said the large barmaid, 'this is the Lounge. The Public's through there.'

The thin man made as if to leave altogether, to walk round the outside of the pub to the correct door. 'You can come through,' said the barmaid, indicating again the connecting door.

'Oh. Thank you. Is that all right?' He began to edge, almost sideways, towards it. 'I like to keep to my own class.'

When he had gone the barmaid stared into space for a moment. So did I, the only occupant of the Lounge except for a quiet couple in the corner. 'I never heard anyone say that,' she said at last, 'I'd better go and see if he's all right,' and bustled out of sight. She came back. 'That's an odd one. Know what he asked for? "Half a pint of the most expensive." '

'Evening Terence.' A regular had entered. 'The usual?'

'You wouldn't try to flog me a pint of that Director's, would you?' Terence appeared an aggressive regular. The barmaid did not respond, drew his pint and said mildly: 'I went to see Billy Graham the other night.'

'Christ!' said Terence.

'That's what he said.' (This was getting good.)

'Typical Yank,' he said.

'I rather liked him. The choir was *lovely*.'

'Oh yes, masses of money.'

'I didn't like the white bucket.'

'Well, it's Yanks isn't it.'

I had to go. I had only been there six minutes and I had heard the subjects nearest the English heart: class (viewed with ambiguous aggression) and the awfulness of foreigners. Also, in the last sequence I had heard two people of opposing view-points discussing something with apparent agreement because

113

neither was listening to the other. This, I take it, is English because it is a sovereign way to avoid an argument. Mr Harold Pinter, to his great credit, was the first to notice this and imitate it on the stage. As a consequence, such conversations, which have gone on forever and all the time, are now known as 'Pinteresque', as though nature imitated art.

I had to go because I was taking part in a charity concert in the church opposite, in aid of the NSPCC. It was a musical concert but I had undertaken to find and read some poems concerned with children. The occasion was complicated by the fact that we had bought some tickets for friends and these, however old and intimate, would need some looking after, whereas all I wanted to do was worry whether I had brought the right pieces of paper.

It was a good concert, with a good choral society and a fine young flautist called Simon Channing. But one of the friends had turned up with flu, the church was extremely draughty, and I feared I was going to have his death on my hands. It is always a mistake to invite friends when one is appearing in public. It affects one's performance. There was a microphone but (not wishing to appear too professionally deft in front of old, sceptical friends) I chose to leave it on and ignore it. As a result, the sculptor Laurence Whitfield told me afterwards, I sounded as though I had a cleft palate or was having trouble with my teeth. (It is always a mistake to invite friends.)

However, after what I took to be an English experience in the pub beforehand, the concert ended with another one. We were invited to join in the choruses of 'Mud, mud, glorious mud', the song by Flanders and Swann. The sight of the choristers, men in dinner jackets, women in long skirts and high, demure blouses, heartily declaring their desire to wallow in mud struck me as the gentility principle in action. There was no farm labourer present, to sing the glories of mud. Have the English middle classes, with that song, found a way of expressing class solidarity, and their Id? Someone should write a thesis about it. And would the French sing 'Boue, boue, boue glorieuse'? Surely something more of the earth, earthy.

2 June 1984

LUDOVIC KENNEDY

A VOYAGE ROUND MY COLON

The consultant and I were looking at an X-ray of my colon. 'Those two white blobs,' he said, 'are polyps. They're quite harmless now but, if we leave them, they could turn nasty later. So you'd best have them out.'

'How long will I be in hospital?' I asked, thinking of days or even weeks away from television and writing.

'A couple of hours or so. We put a tube up your backside. You can see it happening if you want.'

Science marches on. When I'd had the prostate, they'd gone up by another route. But that had kept me in five days: two hours for the polyps was fantastic.

Instructions (called 'Having a Colonoscopy' and with a picture on the front of a cheery-looking doctor waving a piece of paper) reached home a few days later. I was to starve for 36 hours, take a powerful laxative and drink plenty of clear fluids, 'including alcohol if you wish'. So I spent a happy preparatory period in a haze of vodka and tonic.

The rest of the instructions were immensely reassuring. 'When the tube is in place,' they said, 'air will be passed through it to distend the colon and give a clearer view of the lining . . . You may pass some wind but although you may find this embarrassing, remember that staff do understand what is causing it.'

All my life I have done my best not to sound off in company. This *carte blanche* invitation to do so was quite tempting.

On the afternoon of D-Day I was lying in a blue shift on a mobile bed in a room of the Endoscopy Unit of a private clinic (courtesy of PPP). A nurse came in and asked for my X-rays and I remembered I had forgotten them. 'Not to worry,' said the nurse, but I did for a bit, for how else could they find the polyps? Presently a man with greying hair and specs like Douglas Hurd came into the room. 'I'm the doctor who's going to remove your polyps,' he said. He was tremendously joky and jolly, and after he had given me a brief rundown on the life cycle of the polyp, three nurses wheeled me across the corridor and into another room.

In the far corner of this room stood a man in a white coat who looked like Eddie Shah. 'This is a colleague of mine from Cairo,' said the doctor. 'You don't mind if he watches, do you?' I said I'd be delighted. 'You don't have many polyps in Egypt, do you?' asked the doctor, and the man from Cairo said, 'Not in the colon,' though without saying where they did have them.

The nurses turned me on my side and the doctor put a needle into a vein behind my knuckle to make me relaxed. While doing this he gave a wonderful imitation of his coal merchant and his wife. I couldn't decide whether he was doing this to make me even more relaxed, like a warm-up man at a telly show, or because he was over-excited at the prospect of getting at my polyps.

The nurses meanwhile had put the tube in, and now they blew in some air as well. One put her hand on my tummy and pressed and the doctor said, 'Try and do a pooper,' but I couldn't. 'Never mind,' said the doctor, 'now we'll look for the polyps. You can join in too.'

He handed me an eyepiece attached to a long lead and, through a series of prisms, I observed my lower intestines in glorious technicolour. We seemed to be travelling along a sort of miniature pinkish Channel tunnel.

'Ah!' said the doctor gleefully. 'Here's the first one now.' There was no mistaking it was a polyp; bright red like a little cherry, on the end of a long white stalk and swaying gently in the breeze. 'Now watch,' said the doctor, and suddenly a tiny wire loop appeared from nowhere, and with amazing dexterity the doctor lassoed the polyp as if it were a steer. Then he drew the wire tight, applied some heat, and polyp and stalk parted company. 'Like to see it?' he asked, and before you could say 'colonoscopy' it was on a tin tray in front of me, looking very small and battered and sorry for itself.

'That was Father polyp,' said the doctor, and having returned to the chase we located what he called Mother polyp and two baby polyps. One of the baby polyps proved intractable, appearing in the eyepiece one moment, vanishing the next.

'What a coy little polyp you are, for sure,' said the doctor, but he eventually lassoed and dispatched it too. With only one to go, I asked the Cairo doctor if he'd like a dekko down the eyepiece, but he declined – surprisingly, I thought, in view of the shortage of polyps in Egypt.

'That's it!' said the doctor, beaming at me. 'It's all over. Congratulations!' Drowsily I replied, 'Noffer you to gongrashulate me. Me to grashulate you.' But he went on congratulating me all the same.

A week later the consultant rang up. 'Just to tell you,' he said, 'that everything in the colon is now rosy. But we'd like to have another look round there in two years' time.'

'Great!' I said. 'I'll look forward to it.' And I believe I half meant it.

15 February 1986

"Same here, it must be some bug – I feel like death".

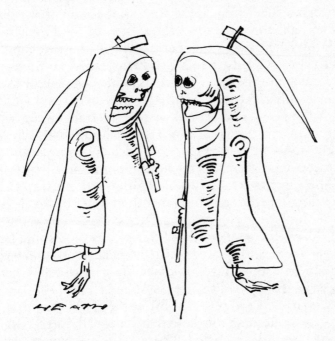

BERNARD LEVIN
(TAPER)

WESTMINSTER COMMENTARY

While the fourteenth Earl of Home was speaking your hawk-eyed correspondent was astonished to see that there were some 140 members present in the House of Lords. Astonished not so much that there are 140 people, even in the British Peerage, willing to listen to the Earl of Home, but that so great a turn-out of the aristocracy should take place for any purpose other than that of ensuring that the right of Englishmen to hang one another by the neck until they are dead should not be tampered with. Nevertheless, there they were, and for nothing more exciting than the Second Reading of the Life Peerages Bill.

Now a bird's-eye view of a large number of Lords is an impressive sight. The first thing one notices is that the proportion of bald pates on the Labour side of the House is substantially higher than on the Tory side: the Tories scored some 22 per cent eggheads, while Labour notched up no less than 40 per cent – and the latter figure did not even include the polished bonce of Earl Attlee, obscured from where I sat by the bulk of Lord Silkin. The Tories made a clean sweep of buttonholes, scoring five (all pink) to Labour's nil. It is unfortunately impossible for me to produce any comparative figures of those who were asleep during some or all of the debate, as nobody has yet been able to devise a satisfactory method of telling whether a member of the House of Lords is conscious or not. (Sir Ivor Jennings's brave theory, adumbrated in his *Cabinet Government* – I think – that you could be sure they were awake if they were actually making a speech has long since gone the way of Bagehot's even more naive belief that they were awake if they had their eyes open.)

So those who had eyes to see, saw. But some of us have ears as well, and it is as spokesman for these that I must advise the Earl of Home to get his radar adjusted. There never was a man who got less on his screen when making a speech. Now his speech, as a matter of fact, was not, as far as his fourteenth Lordship's speeches go, bad at all – though of course his fourteenth Lordship's speeches do not go very far – but for all the 'feel' of his audience that he displayed he might have been as literally deaf as he is metaphorically dumb. Still, he outlined the Government's case on the proposals to create life peers and peeresses, which was after all what he was there for, and the great debate, for which 140 gentlemen of England had turned out on a day so vile that many an heir must have sat expectantly by the telephone as the hours wore on, was under way.

Lord Alexander of Hillsborough, who has the striking distinction of being the only member of the House of Lords who looks even more like a frog than Lord Beaverbrook, replied on behalf of the Opposition, or whatever they call it in the Upper House. Lord A. of H. was by no means entirely at ease (though this can scarcely excuse the way he shouted his head off), since his party has been unable, for twenty-two years, to make up its mind what it wanted to do with, to or about the House of Lords. Having explored the delights of unicameralism, and then found that its need of the House of Lords was even greater than that of the Conservatives, the Labour Party is understandably in a bit of a dither about what to try next. The hereditary system, they have decided, is bad, and the present composition of the House of Lords indefensible. Well, but what to put in its place? Not, clearly, an assembly of ex-directors of the Midland Bank and out-to-grass trade union officials; there are quite enough of both in Another Place. Not – even to the Labour Party's myopic vision – a mish-mash of functional members, with the copper-smelters standing up for the copper-smelting industry and the university professors for the universities. Not a directly elected House, for what would be the point of two identical chambers, particularly since the talent available to stock them is scarcely sufficient for one? And not an indirectly-elected one, as nobody has the remotest idea who then should do the choosing. So Lord Alexander sat on the fence until the horns of his dilemma had entered into his soul, and the Constitution, when he had finished, still stood secure.

Lord Balfour of Burleigh followed him, and said a large

number of things. Since one of them was 'I am quite prepared to concede . . . that his rise to power was aided by elements of the right wing,' the 'his' referring, if you please, to *Hitler*, I do not think I need waste any time on the others. But far though their Lordships were from reality when the debate began, they got farther and farther from it as the hours went by. Bobbity caused many a noble sigh of relief by announcing that he did not intend to vote against the Bill, and turned the sighs of relief into something rather more akin to groans of pain by lambasting the Bill and everything connected with it, including the Earl of Home, whom he ran gently through by saying, 'I cannot look at the position with the same airy optimism that seems to govern the view of the noble Earl the Leader of the House – I have had far too long experience for that.' Indeed, so vigorous was his attack on a Bill which had clearly failed to pass Lord Salisbury's exacting test of legislation – that he should have thought of it first – that Lord Stansgate was moved to ask him why on earth he was going to vote for it.

Soon, delirium set in. 'I am not a normal Peer,' declared the Earl of Airlie with a candidness that did him credit, adding: 'My Lords, the world is moving fast – too fast perhaps – and I should be grateful if your Lordships would not consider this as a platitude; it is a statement of fact' – which indeed it is, as this distracted globe (if the Earl of Home will forgive me) is revolving on its axis at some 1,000 miles per hour, and round the sun at some 62,000. But the eagerly awaited attack on the suggestion that women should be allowed into the House of Lords turned out to be a most amusing and gentle oration, which put its somewhat prehistoric point of view with much good temper and not a little humility. Lord Samuel had ready the blandest retort to an interrupter that I have yet heard: 'I should have been happy to give a conclusive answer to the noble Lord if I had been able to hear him. Unfortunately, I am nowadays immune to interruptions owing to the disabilities of old age.' Lord Lloyd gave me furiously to hope that the Minister of Education had, all unbeknownst to me, been kicked upstairs, and almost convinced me, by the quality of his speech, that I did not hope in vain. Uncle Fred poured oodles of melted butter over their Lordships (who rose to the occasion by looking more and more like sticks of asparagus), while Earl

Ferrers, whom I always thought had been hanged in the early part of the eighteenth century, put the last touches to a day of ripe idiocy by saying that the admission of women would be an unmitigated disaster, owing to the fact that they were organising, pushing and commanding – qualities which I should have thought their Lordships could do with.

Just as my sanity began to sway, Lord Hinchingbrooke suddenly turned up to complete my discomfiture. The fact is, Lord Hinchingbrooke has been following me about these last few days; he turned up at the Law Courts for the libel action against the *Spectator*; I saw him again at Church House during the 'leak' tribunal's first sittings, and now here he was in front of the throne in their Lordships' House. Why, the other day I even saw him in the House of Commons. Perhaps it's all done with mirrors, but however it is done it is very disconcerting, and I will be glad when it stops.

Ah, the House of Commons, madcap, romantic haunt of my youth! They seem to have been discussing for the last ten days nothing but that vital piece of legislation the Isle of Man Bill.

A pall hangs over the House which needs more to account for it than the fog. Overhead the sky is darkened with the shadows of American aeroplanes containing hydrogen-bombs and British aeroplanes containing the Leader of the Opposition. Mr G. will not be back for a month and it is clear that he cannot see any good reason why he should not be away for three. Nor can I; nor can I see any reason why the Prime Minister should not buzz off for a couple of months too, and as a matter of fact he is going to. Why don't they simply pack the whole thing up and let the Isle of Man carry on for a bit longer without its Bill? The most important debate of the week, in either House of Parliament, was a debate in the House of Lords on its own future; the monstrous irrelevance of the entire proceedings seemed positively tasteless. Blindfolded, without apparent purpose, the House of Commons shuffles on this mortal coil; meanwhile the earth, as the Earl of Airlie so cogently implied, spins on its way at 62,000 miles an hour. *Something* will have to happen soon. (Yes, but what?)

6 December 1957

MINIMUM MEAT

Would you let Sir Roy Welensky marry your daughter? (I mean, supposing he wanted to, and all that, naturally.) This pregnant question was shimmering unasked in the air all through Monday's debate on the motion that – well, let's have it in full – 'that the Draft Order in Council, to signify Her Majesty's assent to the Constitutional Amendment Bill of the Federation of Rhodesia and Nyasaland, a copy of which was laid before this House on 31st October, in the last Session of Parliament, be not submitted to Her Majesty.'

Now in considering this question (the one about Sir Roy Welensky, that is, not the one about the Draft Order in Council) we must be entirely calm, and allow ourselves to be swayed only by the dictates of reason. I can make my own position clear at once by saying that, as far as I am concerned, a Welensky is exactly the same as any other man. Indeed, some of my best friends are Welenskies. My old mammy was a Welensky, and a dearer sweeter creature you couldn't hope to find. Many's the time she rocked me to sleep ('Come on, Massa Taper, dey sure do be waitin' for you in de land ob Nod'), and to this day I send her a card every Christmas. And I have enough sense to realise that our lives would be a lot more difficult if it were not for all those useful Welenskies who shine our shoes and serve our meals in railway dining-cars and do the thousand-and-one things that these cheerful, smiling, simple folk do so well.

But, of course, that's not to say that I would like him to marry my daughter. You see, although nobody but a fool (there are such people, I am afraid) would try to maintain that Whites are *inferior* to other people, nobody but a woolly-minded sentimentalist (and there are lots of those about, I regret to say) could deny that they are not *different*. Besides, think of the children – not everybody is as tolerant as me, after all. No, on the whole, I think it best – best for both sides, that is – for the Welenskies to keep themselves to themselves, and my daughter to keep herself to herself.

This, at any rate, seemed to be the sort of feeling that prevailed on the Opposition benches throughout the debate. With one Jim – Callaghan – to open, another – Griffiths – to wind up (suggesting a new collective noun, 'a Jimmage of Socialists'), and a Babs, suffering from a cold, to occupy the middle, not to mention a Mr Dalton to enter during Mr Wade's speech and wind up his watch no fewer than three times in the course of it (a severe but just criticism of Mr Wade's powers of enthralling his audience), the Labour Party was well set to stand, wrapped in Old Glory, as the last bastion against the terrible day when Sir Roy Welensky will overrun the entire country and no woman, not Mrs Castle of the red hair nor Miss Vickers of the blue, will be safe.

What is it about black men that brings out the worst in the Opposition? The Labour Party has an astonishing record of behaving disgracefully to them when in office and making a collective fool of itself about them when out of it. (As for putting anything they say into some kind of operational practice, the West Bromwich busmen may stand as shining examples of the extent to which the idea of the brotherhood of man has actually penetrated into the active consciousness of the rank and file, or at any rate of the extent to which they are willing to exercise anything but their lower jaws in pursuit of it.) The first fact that emerges from even a cursory study of the provisions of the Constitutional Amendment Bill is that when it has been passed more Africans will have the vote than have it now, and there will be more African members of the Federation's legislatures than there are at the moment. Now admittedly this could hardly be expected to satisfy the *Observer*, which sometimes gives the impression that it will only be completely happy when there isn't a white face to be seen on a legislative bench from Woolloomooloo to Westminster, but the Labour Party, which is, after all, supposed to operate within the confines of the inevitability of gradualness, really ought to know better.

Yet you should have heard Mr Dugdale, for instance, when he was may-the-Lord-have-mercy-on-your-souling around for nearly half an hour. Talking of the qualifications necessary for Africans if they are to be admitted to the franchise, he said this:

> What strange standards of civilisation and responsibility these are, based on the ownership of property or on a minimum income. Does the Minister consider that Gandhi was a less civilised person than Henry Ford? On the Minister's basis, he quite plainly would have been. What about Keir Hardie? Was he less civilised than the Duke of Westminster? Under this system Keir Hardie would not have had a vote. [Nor does the Duke of Westminster, cully.] . . .
>
> During the course of European civilisation there have been many poor writers, scientists, artists and musicians who have contributed much to it. Yet such men as Rembrandt, who was in the bankruptcy court, and Mozart, who was given a pauper's burial, would be regarded as uncivilised and not worthy of having a vote on these standards . . . they are simply a device to keep Africans from getting the vote . . .

Honestly, it's enough to shake even my faith in the wisdom of our legislators. What have Gandhi and Mozart and Rembrandt to do with the question? Because Rembrandt went bankrupt are bankrupts in general therefore admirable men? Because Mozart was given a pauper's burial should all dead paupers in Nyasaland therefore be given the vote? Because Gandhi fasted in pursuit of his religious or political beliefs should the government of the Federation be handed over to all Africans who can show they have bad digestions? You might just as well say that because Sir Reginald Manningham-Buller is one of the occupants of the Government front bench, Mr Dugdale should be given ministerial office if the Labour Party manages to win the next election.

I would give the Labour Party credit, if I could, for not believing the nonsense it talked during this debate, but I fear it was all too sincere. The air of unreality was, so to speak, quite real. They decided – and the decision was itself significant – to spend a whole day trying to slow down the already slow progress towards some kind of racial good sense in Central Africa, and they failed only because the Tories happen to have more members than the Opposition. One day the reverse may be the case, but I think we can trust West Bromwich hypocrisy to do a Seretse Khama when it comes to the point. Of course, if they had anything more sensible to talk about there would be no need for them to create this kind of carry-on, but once again their failure to nerve themselves for the fray and indeed to find something concrete to fray about was all too sharply demonstrated. There is a permanent end-of-session pall hanging over Westminster today, in which nobody has anything to say or suggest, in which the Government reels from one fumble to another, and the Opposition beats the air, and tempers, having been quite in abeyance for weeks on end, suddenly snap, and a lot of people without enough to occupy their minds spend rather too much time giggling.

It will, I trust, be generally agreed that the only remotely intelligent, interesting or important question of the week was Mr Norman Dodds's request to have a minimum meat-content for sausages laid down by law. Most of the sausages bought in this country are made of bread, low-grade synthetic rubber, unusable seed potatoes, very old sump-oil, typewriter ribbons, export-rejected rexine chair-covers and imperfectly repulped

telegraph forms, and the sooner somebody compels the manufacturers at any rate to wave a pig's trotter somewhere near the
mixing-machine, the better most of us will be pleased. But
anyone who has even been in the House of Commons when the
Kitchen Committee was reporting will know what happened
when Mr Dodds asked Question No. 18. Hundreds of grown
men and women collapsed, many of them in unseemly
positions, and laughed till they damn near bust their waistcoat
buttons. The Patronage Secretary, who would laugh, I verily
believe, if someone dropped a guillotine blade on the back of his
neck from a great height, surpassed himself; I really thought he
was going to have a seizure. Of course, they must relax; but it
looks as if the part of their anatomy with which they think has
become so relaxed it will no longer function at all.

Yet here we are, barely half-way through the legal life of this
Parliament, and apparently quite ready to keep it going for
most, if not all, of the second half. They will never get there at
this rate; everybody will have died of boredom long before the
day of release. It is mainly due, of course, to the fact that the
Labour Party has only the merest fragment of a policy and finds
it difficult to become enthusiastic about that, while the
Government has no idea of how to get through any trouble that
may lie ahead apart from burning incense and making the
appropriate sign to ward off the evil eye. But looming larger
than one may think is the fact that running the machine these
days has become at the same time so physically strenuous and
mentally enervating that most of them are bound to be played
out long before five years have passed. Good gracious, suppose
the Chartists were right!

29 November 1957

ZENGA LONGMORE

CHATTING UP TECHNIQUES

As a young black woman, travelling around southern Africa with my white stepbrother, I was chatted up from Zimbabwe to Botswana, straight through to Lesotho, and on to Jo'burg. I have here compiled a study of the chatting up techniques of the Shona (western Zimbabwe), Ndebele (eastern Zimbabwe), Tswana (Botswana), Masotho (Lesotho), and the Boer (no explanation necessary).

Study I: the Shona
Setting: Harare Gardens
Shona: (In posh suit) Em – er – em, excuse me, madame.
Me: Yes?
Shona: I'm so sorry to disturb you madame, but I thought you looked a little confused.
Me: No, I'm fine.
Shona: That is good, madame, but you see, it is not often you see a white lady on her own in Harare.
Me: White?
Shona: Oh yes madame, of *course* you are white.
Me: No I'm not. If I was, would you be coming up to talk to me?
Shona: Well, actually, no, I would not, madame, but you are almost white, I can assure you. Where are you from?
Me: England.
Shona: England: what a lovely place, madame. The English are very good people. What is your name?
Me: Ethel.
Shona: My name is Jeff (or John). I am an accountant. Are you – em – are you married?
Me: Yes. (Or no, depending on how good looking he is.)
Shona: Could I please have your address, madame, so that I may correspond with you in London. It is such an honour to meet you.

(At this point I make an excuse and leave – or not, as the case may be)

N.B. The fortunate ones who acquire my address, write to tell me that meeting me was like meeting Princess Anne. I decided, after hours of tortuous debate, to be flattered.

Study II the Ndebele

Setting: dingy bar in Bulawayo

Me: (Chatting to barman)

Ndebele: (To barman) Hey, what are you doing chatting to a vulnerable young woman who's all on her own in a strange country. She's not going to think there are any gentlemen left in Zimbabwe – you *are* all on your own, aren't you?

Me: Yep.

Ndebele: (Hurriedly sitting next to me) Thought so. Look at you! so prim and proper, and fenced in. Relax! You're in Africa now! Be like me, laid back and cool.

Me: Nope.

Ndebele: Still, you can always be tutored I suppose. Come to the Ambassadors Night Spot with me, now. Hurry up, I don't have time to waste.

Me: Nope.

Ndebele: Don't give me that: I know your sort, too posh for me, eh?

Me: (Leaving in a marked manner) Yep.

(I didn't like Bulawayo much)

Study III the Tswana

Setting: some bar or other

Tswana: (Wearing bright tee shirt and jeans) Heh! Dumela me.

Me: Khotso ntate.

Tswana: So how is Ramotswa these days, sis?

Me: I'm not from Ramotswa, I'm from England.

Tswana: You are lying! You are from Ramotswa! Think I can't spot a Ramotswa woman when I see one!

Me: B-b-but . . .

Tswana: Ah yes, the English accent. Very clever – but you don't fool me. I too can put on an English accent. (Puts on high falsetto voice in exactly the same accent.) 'How *do* you *DO*' See! Anyway, I don't mind. I often tell lies myself.

Me: But it's the truth.

Tswana: Well, whatever you are, I like your style, ossi. Now, don't you dare tell me you're married.

Me: No.

Tswana: Eh! EEEEH! And I know you like jazz because I saw you at the jazz festival last night. So I'll see you there tonight. Eeee!

(Calls friends over, and everyone drinks and jokes, someone'll bung on a radio, and everyone will dance in the hot sun. BLISS. I wasn't with my brother much in Botswana, so there was much time for such escapades.)

Study IV the Masotho

Setting: an outside cafe

Enter staggeringly handsome Masotho, wearing blanket and Basotho hat.

S.H. Masotho: U tsohile joang?

Me: Ja what?

S.H. Masotho: (In faltering English) From where are you?

Me: England.

S.H. Masotho: I thought you were Indian. Your name, ma?

Me: Zenga – and you?

S.H. Masotho: My name is Staggeringly Handsome Masotho (or whatever). How long you stay in Lesotho?

Me: Only five days unfortunately.

S.H. Masotho: Five days, ah, not long enough (giving wickedly handsome smile). But if you like, ma, I could take you to the – (Enter brother)

S.H. Masotho: Your husband?

Me: No! My brother!

S.H. Masotho: Ah no, I think he is your husband (looking nervous).

Me: (Becoming desperate as he leaves) No! I SWEAR he's my brother! You see our mother is half-Russian, and half-Danish, his father is English, my father is – hey! Come back. Where are you going? You said you were going to take me to the –

(But he's gone, looking at my brother and backing away. I shall have to go alone next year.)

Study V the Boer

Me: (Going into a toilet).
Boer: Heh! Can't you read?
(Points at notice saying: 'WHITES ONLY! NICHT FOR BLECKS'.) I think you'll agree that the Boer lacks a certain *je ne sais quoi*.

26 October 1985

FERDINAND MOUNT

A TALE OF TWO INNER CITIES

'I'm Oliver Twist's new case worker. Oliver, I have come to take you back into care.'

'Yes, Miss.' Oliver looked in awe at this woebegone young female with her huge spectacles and her lank wisps of hair. Nothing less like a suitcase could possibly be imagined. Perhaps she kept a suitcase at home, or hundreds of suitcases and slept in a different one every night. Or perhaps she would shut *him* up in a suitcase, along with dozens of newborn babies in overnight grips and waifs locked in Gladstone bags.

'You must not call me Miss. You must call me Brunnhilde.'

But poor Oliver there and then resolved that he could no more address this strange Suitcase Worker by the mysterious appellation of Brown Hilda than fly to the moon, so he fell quiet and gazed at the floor. And such a floor it was too, such a cracked, greasy, coffee-stained square of linoleum that a cockroach would have twisted its ankle trying to cross it. There were stubs of Brown Hilda's cigarettes all over it, wall to wall. Why, the very carpet-sweeper must have chocked to death on it. The soles of your shoes would catch lung cancer in a minute.

'Please Miss, I want some more.'

'I never knew such a greedy boy. You've only just finished your Diet Salad. In Sweden, all the little boys and girls love their Diet Salad.'

But Oliver was dreaming of the fat sugary doughnuts with runny jam which he had had with Mr Brownlow, and the delicious burgers with steaming processed cheese spilling over the sides, and the pizzas with extra peperoni and onions, and the Big Macs with their glorious forbidden taste of fatty cardboard. And then there were the piping hot dinners in the workhouse, the mounds of soggy golden French fries, and the steak and kidney pies and the heaps of spaghetti soused in ketchup. And tears rolled down Oliver's cheeks at the thought of the bygone days with the dear old Bumbles: the skiing trip when Mr Bumble had got so drunk, the pony-trekking holiday in Wales with Marlene Bumble. But now the workhouse had been turned into artists' studios, and only the Bumbles lingered on in the caretaker's flat, complaining about the damp.

'So this is the boy.' A plump, oleaginous personage in clerical habit peered down at Oliver. 'You say he is maladjusted, Miss Lundqvist?'

'He does not find it easy to form stable relationships, Mr Chadband.'

'He is an orphan of the Inner Cities. And what are the Inner Cities, my friends? Are they a vale of health? No, they are not. Are they a place of resort for decent folk? No, my friends, they are not. They are an abode of dee-priv-ayshun. This is a dee-prived boy. Watch him, Miss Lundqvist, watch him well.'

But Brown Hilda did not watch him at all, because she had other occupations to pursue. She had her odd little cigarettes to roll which had such a sweet foreign smell to them, and she had telephone calls to make, oh such a lot of telephone calls. I swear the managing director of British Telecom called on her every Christmas with two dozen red roses to thank her for her custom.

So Oliver ran away down the Seven Sisters Road, doubled round the Sainsburys in the Holloway Road, dodged the juggernauts at Highbury Corner and found himself panting like a puppy in front of Mr Brownlow's commodious villa in Pentonville. But hallo, what was this? Boards up, For Sale, 'Gone away, had to sell up,' said a passer-by muffled to the eyes against the wind-chill factor. 'They say he was a Name at Lloyds.' And Oliver wept at the thought of his good old benefactor, reduced to nothing but a name, bankrupted of flesh and blood, a pale wandering nominative.

'What have we here? Boy blubbing in the street. Are you giving me an audition, boy, trying to extort my sympathy, hey?'

'No sir. Why should I be?'

'Don't you know who I am, boy?' roared a highly portentous gentleman in a veritable echo chamber of a voice.

'Are you on television Sir?' quavered Oliver.

'Certainly not, boy. I despise and reject the idiot box. I am the last survivor of the live the-atre. Vincent Crummles of Crummles Peoples Productions at your service, a poor wandering player clinging on by the grace of God and the Arts Council. Do you want to be an Act-or, boy?'

'Not specially Sir.'

'Quite right, dear boy. It's a diabolically overcrowded profession. No standing room. We can only take half-a-dozen boys a year from the Donald Sinden School for Overacting, keen as mustard, fees all paid by the Manpower Services Commission, did the entire Wars of the Roses last season, didn't cost me a penny. Come and meet the Infant Phenomenon.'

'Can it, Dad,' retorted an extremely short young lady in pink dungarees. 'My name's Ninetta, and I'm a Person of Restricted Growth, and I'll report you to the Equal Height Commission if you don't watch your language.'

'It's not like the old days,' Mr Crummles said mournfully, sniffing a pinch of some powder which Oliver thought did not look very like Mr Brownlow's snuff. 'We used to put on well-made plays then – *Private Lives, The Deep Blue Sea, Dial M for Murder*. But now it's all Pinter and Brecht and Beckett if you want your grant. Not a decent love scene in a single one of them. Nothing for Mrs Crummles to get her teeth into. If you're looking for work, dear boy, you could always try the people who used to do our costumes before there was a slight unpleasantness about the bill.'

And so, tired and dejected, Oliver made his way through the warren of lanes north of Oxford Street, past angry men wheeling racks of clothes swathed in polythene, to ring the bell at the neat block of offices just off Cavendish Square.

'That demd bell,' he heard a voice scream. 'Don't answer it, my poppet. Let it ring, light of my heart. I simply can't see a demnition soul. If it's the media, tell them that Mantalini is holding exploratory talks with Habitat-Mothercare and that the reverse take-over of Laura Ashley is off until the Harrods deal has been to the Office of Fair Trading.'

Oliver sighed and turned away and directed his flagging footsteps to the one place in this harsh world where he knew he would always be welcome.

'Why Oliver, my boy, come in, come in. The bubbly is on

the video, help yourself, my dear. Mr Sikes here was just telling us about his little brush with the law.'

'So I says to them, ladies and gentlemen of the jury, I says, and you *are* ladies and gentlemen within the meaning of the Act, because you have done your duty, you have stood up for the right of your true-born Englishman to protect his castle against intruders.'

'But, Bill, you was the intruder.'

'That was a mere technicality, you old skinflint. I never wanted to blow him away. You know me, Fagin, I only take the shooter along for form's sake. These days my main interests are in financial services. Now about this here Business Expansion Scheme, if young Oliver can do the shinning up the drain-pipe . . .'

But Oliver was already fast asleep on the zebra-skin sofa-bed. And God bless us every one, in a very real sense.

21/28 December 1985

"But I thought they built the M25 so we wouldn't have to see that sort of thing".

SHIVA NAIPAUL

ZAMBIA'S COMPROMISE WITH THE WEST

I became alarmed when, without the slightest hesitation, the New Zealander with whom I had been travelling (and New Zealand, it ought to be recalled, was, at that time, in official disfavour throughout black Africa because of its recent rugby tour of South Africa) told the immigration official at the Tanzanian-Zambian border post of Tunduma that he was intending to travel in transit through Zambia on his way to South Africa. I was amazed at his foolhardy naïveté. After all, Zambia is among the foremost of the 'front-line' states supposedly locked in battle with the white-supremacist South. Kenneth Kaunda, one imagines (or is led to imagine), is made of sterner stuff than, say, Seretse Khama of Botswana – another 'front-line' President – who, when he recently fell ill, was rushed off for treatment at a 'whites only' hospital in Johannesburg.

And so my surprise was great when, without comment, the passport was stamped and returned with a smile. At the very least, I had expected him to receive some sort of lecture, or reprimand. Even more surprisingly, the officer then went on, in the most obliging way possible, to suggest the alternative routes (through Zambia) he could have taken to 'Jo'burg', thus saving himself time and money and trouble.

I soon learned not to be surprised at this permissive attitude. On the contrary: I soon learned to be surprised at any display of its *opposite*. Rhodesia and South Africa, the traveller soon discovers, arouse more passion in the West than they do among the citizenry of the black 'front-line' states. The shelves of one Lusaka supermarket I went into were laden with South African merchandise – meat, toilet paper, detergent, tinned goods of all kinds. In former days, apparently, the source of origin used to be disguised. Nowadays, no one bothers to take the trouble. As I strolled along the alleyways of that Lusaka supermarket, I reflected ruefully on the crises of conscience occasioned in the past by my consumption of South African oranges.

The Rhodesian question provokes irritation rather than altruistic sentiments. The irritation was rampant in the young clerk who complained to me about the steep rise that had occurred in the cost of living. He was, like all town-based Zambian males – and despite his declared poverty – flamboyantly attired: his shoes were platformed, his trousers flared, his red corduroy jacket exquisitely waisted, his tie exceedingly broad and colourful. He did not attribute his poverty to the fall in the price of copper – which earns for Zambia the bulk of its foreign exchange – but laid the blame on the support the Government was giving to the 'liberation struggle'. 'The Ministers are all right – they are rich men. The freedom fighters are all right – they get free food. But what about people like us who are not Ministers and not freedom fighters? They should look after us *first*.' Did he not, then, support the aims of the freedom fighters? He laughed. 'How can a man on seventy-five *kwacha* a month [one kwacha is roughly equivalent to one dollar] support anything? My stomach comes first!'

I sympathised: Lusaka is one of the most expensive cities in the world. Zambia's finances are so bad that the salaries of civil servants are often in arrears; the university is unable to buy books to stock its libraries; cigarettes are in short supply because the manufacturers have no foreign exchange to purchase the necessary packaging materials. When the copper markets sneeze, Zambia catches pneumonia. Many of the youthful unemployed and underemployed of Lusaka gaze with longing towards Rhodesia. Several of those I spoke to said they would – if they could – go there to seek work. Naturally, the Zambian government cannot allow that. If it *did* it would, of course, be behaving no differently from the government of another 'front-line' state – Mozambique. The economy of Mozambique would probably collapse if the government did not allow substantial numbers of its citizens to work in the mines of South Africa.

As is the case all over East and Central Africa, it is not the whites who arouse the greatest animosity, but the Asians. (Whites arouse no animosity at all really. In this part of the world, when Africans and Europeans talk about 'racial harmony' they mean always racial harmony between black and white. History has shown that it is the brown man who invariably pays the price whenever black and white decide to put aside their antagonisms.) My stay coincided with a vigorous anti-Asian campaign in the Zambian press. Day after day, in the *Times* of Zambia, lengthy articles and impassioned letters to the editor were devoted to this enthralling subject. Asian women were accused of harbouring feelings of superiority because they did not sleep with or marry Zambian men. Photographs were published showing suitcases filled to the brim with bank notes allegedly seized from Asians attempting to smuggle currency out of the country. Asian businessmen, predictably enough, were guilty of monopolising the distributive trades and exploiting innocent Zambians. Could Asians, one letter-writer wanted to know, ever become patriots? Peasants, seething with righteous indignation, fired the crops on Asian-owned farms in the eastern part of the country. The climax came with the front page headline which read: 'Asian doctors kill their patients.' It was an open secret, an Assembly woman said, that Indians could buy their medical degrees on the streets of Bombay. They then came all the way to countries like Zambia to practise their deadly art on unsuspecting black men.

I travelled by road from Dar-es-Salaam to Lusaka with a party of Australians, New Zealanders and Americans, most of whom were on their way 'South'. They were all young – none past their middle twenties – and curiously apathetic: they slept through some of the most spectacular Tanzanian scenery. I remarked on this to one of them – a blond, curly-headed American boy, the darling of the girls in the party. 'I'm not really interested in Africa or Africans as such,' he replied with disarming frankness. Why, then, had he come to Africa? To sort out, he said, some 'emotional problems'. Apparently, there was a girl back home in California, concerning whom he 'could not make up his mind'. He showed me her photograph. 'She's no Greta Garbo,' he admitted, staring critically at the photograph. 'Still, she's got some really admirable qualities.' But, I pressed, why come all the way to Africa to sort out his emotional problems? Why not Mexico? 'I came to see the wild life,' he said, assuming a most earnest expression. 'I *care* a great deal about the wild life.' As he talked about his 'concern' for the elephant, I remembered the Swede I had met in Dar-es-Salaam.

European influence, he declared to me one day, had wreaked terrible damage in Africa. This, in itself, was a not particularly arresting proposition. All the same, I asked what aspect of European influence had, in his opinion, done the most harm. 'The introduction of Western medicine,' he answered without hesitation. Modern medicine had, by increasing the number of Africans, ruined the ecological balance. 'The result is that you have a lot more Africans competing with the game. It's not the animals we should be putting in reservations. It's the blacks.'

Late one night we camped near an embankment of the Chinese railway. After we had eaten, the men of the party sat around the fire. Keith, another of the Americans, asked Ian, our New Zealand driver and acknowledged African expert, what Rhodesia was like.

'Fantastic,' Ian said. 'Bloody fantastic. It's the *cleanest* country I've ever been in. Maybe Switzerland is just as clean. I can't say. But Rhodesia . . .'

'Switzerland is pretty clean,' Keith said.

Ian began telling of a public toilet he had once patronised in Bulawayo. So clean was it, he could see his face in the brass fittings. 'They employ two or three coons on a full-time basis to keep it that way. I tell you, man, I've never seen a toilet like that anywhere else, not even in South Africa. It's so clean you feel it's a crime to use it.'

Keith stirred and poked the fire with a stick. 'You think the coons will ever take over there?'

'I figure they might,' Ian said. 'But it will be the biggest bloody tragedy that's ever happened. What's more, the coons won't like it either.'

'What's South Africa like?' It was the boy with emotional problems who spoke. 'Is it as bad as some people make it out to be?'

'A weird and wonderful place,' Ian said. 'I think I prefer Rhodesia, though. The kaffirs might be as thick as glue. But some of those Afrikaners take the cake.'

'They say it's a beautiful country,' Keith said.

'The most beautiful place you'll see this side of heaven,' Ian said. 'What a mind-bending place. I once saw a guy walk up to another guy and stab him in the eye – just like that.'

'Wow!' The boy with emotional problems shivered and hugged his knees.

'That must have been quite something,' Keith said. He looked pale and haggard in the firelight. He was still recovering from an atack of malaria; an attack he had quite deliberately courted by refusing ('Now,' I had heard him say, 'I can tell the folks back home that I had malaria *in Africa*') to take any of the usual prophylactics. 'And was one guy white and the other black?' he asked.

'No, no,' Ian said. 'Both were kaffirs. The fuzz didn't give a damn. A weird and wonderful place is Jo'burg.'

'Sounds a bit like America,' the boy with emotional problems said. 'Do you know that Washington DC is almost eighty per cent black? Jeez! *The capital of the United States!* Can you imagine that? Coons everywhere you look.'

A train, its headlamps sweeping the dark like searchlights, rattled along the embankment. We had been three full days on the road; and Lusaka was still some three hundred miles away.

The Zambian landscape is one note endlessly repeated. At the Tunduma frontier the character of the land suddenly changes. The rolling hills of south-central Tanzania fade away and the table-flat upland of the Zambian plateau begins. Open grassy country gives way to derelict woodland; a featureless wilderness of spindly trees, twenty to thirty feet in height. Mile after mile, hour after hour, it remains the same. Occasionally, a low range of hills is glimpsed in the far distance, but their promise of release from the hypnotic monotony is deceptive. Their summits reveal nothing – nothing but the woolly canopy of the wilderness stretching away on all sides as far as the eye can see. Heat waves dance on the mirror-like asphalt. Now and then, in a clearing in the bush, there is the fleeting apparition of a village of mud huts. Women, squatting in the shade, look up expressionlessly from their labours; squads of naked children, shouting, arms flailing, come rushing over the beaten brown earth to wave at the lorry. The wilderness closes in again. You doze, you wake up, you doze once more. Ahead, unwinding to a destination that seems increasingly unreal, the black ribbon of unswerving asphalt disappears over the crest of a rise in the middle distance; only to reappear on the summit of another, more remote acclivity. Nothing indicates that you have made any progress. You wait for some sort of resolution – the physical catharsis of a towering mountain, a rushing river, a blossoming of the unrelenting woodland into human cultivation. But there is no resolution, no release from the delirious sameness.

In some places the land was on fire, tongues of orange flame licking through the dry undergrowth. Banks of billowing smoke shrouded the blackened skeletons of burnt-out trees. Ash covered the ground like snow. Hordes of white butterflies, whirling dizzily around the lorry, immolated themselves on the radiator and windscreen; or were crushed under the wheels. At sunset, the land was a sullen, smoking desolation, the tepid air soured with the acrid odours of smouldering vegetation. Sometimes the road followed the Chinese railway. It was a strange sight. With its neat stone and iron bridge, its tidily gravelled embankments, it looked as dainty and as functionless as a child's toy. Occasionally, there were 'stations', brand new, pink-washed block houses with their names printed in large letters. But these stations, opening on to untenanted bush, were no more than their names; seeds of unspecified hope scattered in the Zambian wastes. Zambia, with an area of nearly 300,000 square miles, contains fewer than five million people. The country is one of the most sparsely populated in the world. Lusaka is, in a sense, merely a scaled-up version of those toy stations planted in the bush. There is, so far as it is possible to tell, no specially compelling reason for its being where it is. Suddenly, it looms up on the horizon, its skyscrapers silhouetted against the blank Central African sky.

In Kenya the official state philosophy goes under the name of 'Harambee'. (It is, strictly speaking, more of a slogan than a 'philosophy'.) It is a Swahili word meaning 'pull together' and is used to denote the national idea of 'self-help' – or 'help yourself' as one cynic remarked to me. In Tanzania the official state philosophy is, of course, 'African socialism' as expressed by the ujamaa communes. Zambia, not to be outdone, has its own unique philosophy, elaborated by its President, Kenneth Kaunda. He calls it 'Humanism'.

'It means,' a Lusaka police inspector told me, 'that here in Zambia we put Man at the centre of things.' I asked him to be a little more precise. 'Well,' he said, after thinking hard for a while, 'the colour of your skin is not the same colour as the colour of my skin. Do you agree?' I agreed. 'That's it, you see!'

I looked at him perplexedly. My obtuseness obviously saddened him. 'Well,' he said, 'you agreed that the colour of my skin is different from the colour of your skin. Would you also agree that we are friends?' I said I would like to think that we were – even though we had met less than an hour ago. 'That's it, you see! That's exactly it! Although my colour is different from yours, it doesn't stop me being your friend. And that is because I am a *humanist*. Do you understand now?' I said I understood a little better – but not fully. How, for instance, did Zambian humanism differ from Tanzanian socialism which also claimed that it put Man at the centre of things? 'Here in Zambia,' he replied, 'we are not so militant as they are in Tanzania. I would say we are about two-thirds socialistic. Here we have something like ujamaa but we call it by a different name. We call it village regrouping.'

Zambia's humanism is, if anything, even harder to pin down than Tanzania's rival – or perhaps complementary – state ideology. The Lusaka intelligentsia are hardly any more enlightening than my friend, the police inspector. 'Zambian humanism,' one of them declared, as if reading from a prepared statement, 'aims at eradicating all evil tendencies in Man.' Its ultimate goal, he went on, is nothing less than 'the attainment of Human Perfection' which will be achieved by ridding society of 'negative human inclinations such as selfishness, greed, hypocrisy, individualism, laziness, racism, tribalism, provincialism, nationalism, colonialism, neo-colonialism, fascism, poverty, disease, ignorance and exploitation of man by man.' He gazed at me breathlessly. When that comprehensive programme of social renovation has been completed – and, under the wise and inspired leadership of President Kaunda, it was already well under way in Zambia – the people would live by the dictates of Love. Such things as prisons and police forces would become utterly irrelevant. I mentioned these hopes to the police inspector. 'It looks,' I said, 'as if you'll soon be out of a job.' He laughed. 'I think it will be some time before *that* happens,' he said, and happily poured himself – and me – yet another beer.

Beer is a major – some say *the* major – obsession of the Zambian people. Zambia, so the rumour runs, is second only to Australia in per capita consumption of the beverage. Another

rumoured statistic, with which the first may not be uncon-
nected, is that Zambia boasts the highest per capita road-
accident rate in the world – though I happen to think that the
mesmerising monotony of the landscape must also be an
important contributing factor. However, it is the remarkable
consumption of beer, not the mangled vehicles abandoned on
the roadsides, which first impresses itself on the visitor.
Zambians, young and old, male and female, rich and poor,
drink with a dedication I have rarely seen surpassed. When my
friend, the police inspector, ordered what he called a 'round', it
consisted of six bottles; and *his* round was followed by *my*
round. With certain individuals dedication becomes naked
worship. I have watched a woman, her eyes closed in ecstatic
surrender, her head thrown back, sucking at the mouth of a
bottle with all the world-oblivious contentment of a baby at its
mother's breast. I did not witness that tableau on the street but
in the bar of the not unrespectable hotel where I was staying.

Late one evening I stopped for the night at a township in
central Zambia. The manager of the single shabby 'hotel'
greeted me with the sad news that there was no beer. My
companion at dinner was a disgruntled captain of the Zambian
Air Force. 'They're fighting in the town over beer,' he said.
'The people are sad and miserable. This is not fair. The Minister
should be told. It shouldn't be like this at all.' He levelled his
fork at me. 'They said they were going to pay special attention
to the rural areas. I know for a fact that in Lusaka they have over
a hundred bars. Here we have five. Five! I don't call that paying
attention to rural areas.' Some weeks earlier a Zambian
delegation had been to West Germany on a 'goodwill' tour. As
was only to be expected, they paid particular attention to the
German brewing industry. An account of the visit was
published in the *Times* of Zambia. 'In Bavaria,' the writer,
Stephen Mpofu, tells his readers, 'traditional beer – their
version of our own *Kachasu* – is popular with drinkers . . . it is
made by monks from roots collected for them by villagers from
the bush . . .'

The state-run television service clamours for abstinence in
between its canned American and British 'shows'. How can
Rhodesia be liberated if we Zambians spend so much of our
time and money drinking beer? How can the humanist society

take shape? Beer, selling for between seven and ten shillings a bottle, is not cheap by Zambian or any other standards. Nevertheless, despite the price, despite the complaints about the cost of living, Zambians still seem to find the money to buy it – just as they seem to be able to find the money to indulge in their other great obsession: clothes.

The expatriate lecturer in English (expatriates staff the mines, the medical services, the factories, the schools, the technical colleges – without them, the country would fall apart) waved apologetically at the handful of books, perhaps half-a-dozen, on the library shelf. 'There,' he said, 'that's it. That's all the Zambian literature there is.' For him, the paucity is a source of genuine embarrassment. 'I would dearly love to teach something Zambian to my students. But what can I do if there's nothing?' (The dearth, though, does not necessarily breed humility; the same lecturer was attacked by one of his students for teaching Shakespeare on the grounds that he was a 'white writer'.) The man who writes a book in Zambia is immediately whisked away into the higher reaches of the administration. One of the writers represented on the shelf had become a member of the Central Committee of the Party; another had become head of a large state-owned organisation. But, with the fruits of high office dangling so alluringly before them, Zambia is by no means short of would-be writers. I met one of these. He was, at the time, working for a company producing mainly educational books.

'The book I am writing,' he said, 'is highly symbolic. It's a story about maize, white ants and black ants.'

I asked what the maize was supposed to symbolise.

'The maize symbolises the people. I believe the white ants and the black ants speak for themselves.'

'What's the story line?'

'To begin with I show how the white ants come and eat up the maize. Then I show how the black ants decide to form an army. They come along eventually and eat up the white ants.'

'And what happens after that?'

He seemed surprised by the question. 'Nothing happens after that.'

'That's the end of the story?'

'Of course.'

'After eating up the white ants, aren't the black ants tempted to eat up the maize?'

'No, no, no.' he laughed. 'How can the black ants eat up the maize? They've come to *save* the maize. No, no, no.' He became serious again. 'After I finish that book I intend to write another one.'

'Will that be symbolic too?'

'Of course.'

'What will the symbols be?'

'Mainly spiders.'

'Spinning symbolic webs and so on?'

'Of course.'

11 June 1977

"It's not fair!"

NOTEBOOK

*Short pieces by Christopher Booker, Alexander Chancellor,
Christopher Fildes, John Grigg, Richard Ingrams, Charles
Moore, Keith Waterhouse, Alan Watkins, Richard West, A. N.
Wilson and Peregrine Worsthorne.*

CHRISTOPHER BOOKER

I am still trying to puzzle out the most complicated mixed
metaphor yet thrown up by this year's party conference season
– David Steel's warning that 'we must not put on the shoulders
of the Monarch the strain of picking up the pieces behind a pack
of politicians determined to pursue party advantage in splendid
isolation and attempting to seize the blank cheque of Prime
Ministership'. Would candidates please attempt to draw what is
going on, using one side of the paper.

28 September 1985

ALEXANDER CHANCELLOR

The English, when they are away from home, seem to be
obsessed with going to the lavatory. They are constantly on the
prowl for 'toilets', and their needs seem to be well catered for by
local authorities, as large signposts saying 'Toilet' can be found
in even the remotest corners of the countryside. It is clearly a
problem which nobody can risk ignoring. A good little article
in Tuesday's *Evening Standard* advising readers of the attractions of Chartwell, Sir Winston Churchill's former home in
Kent, concludes with the triumphant announcement: 'There
are extensive public lavatories in the grounds.'

19 August 1978

The gossip columnists made a meal of the *Spectator*'s 150th anniversary party last week, so you may feel that enough has been written about it. But there were two incidents which I feel deserve reporting. The first was a conversation at the bar between myself, the bandleader, and the *Spectator*'s distinguished columnist, Mr Patrick Marnham. It went as follows: *Me* (speaking somewhat indistinctly): 'May I introduce Tommy Hawkins, the leader of the band. This is Patrick Marnham, the greatest writer in England.' *Marnham*: 'You are a very good bandleader.' *Hawkins* (very politely): 'I am sure you are also an excellent waiter.' Second incident. As I walked down the Strand at 5.00 am on my way home I was approached by a young man trying to sell me a copy of our 150th anniversary issue. He had been at the party and removed an armful of the copies which had been supplied free for guests. When I told him that I had a copy, that I was the Editor of the *Spectator* etcetera, he became very embarrassed and tried to press on me a pound note which, he said, were his takings so far – not bad at 5.00 am in the Strand. But of course I did not accept it. Such initiative deserves its reward. Incidentally, I should apologise to Mrs Sheila Burns of Kingswood in Surrey who has written to me complaining about the party. 'It would seem,' she says, 'that the only people missing from this fantastic affair were the poor bloody infantry – the readers. I can't tell you why but I'm damned annoyed.' I should perhaps reassure Mrs Burns that, contrary to widespread opinion, we do actually have more readers than can be comfortably accommodated in the Lyceum Theatre.

30 September 1978

Graham Greene, so it is said, once won a *Spectator* competition with a parody of his own work. It was partly in the hope that he might attempt to do so again that in April 'Jaspistos' set a similar competition asking for an extract from an imaginary Greene novel. There was a large number of entries, some of them extremely good. But was any one of them from Greene himself? The winning entry was sent in under the name of Sebastian Eleigh. Sebastian Eleigh, we have established, was none other than Graham's younger brother, Sir Hugh Greene. In third place was a contribution from a certain Katharine

Onslow, who, so it turns out, was in fact Graham's sister, Mrs Elisabeth Dennys. So the family acquitted itself remarkably well. But what of Graham? We felt sure that he had entered. Our suspicions, for a number of good reasons, came to rest upon an entry under the name of Colin Bates, which, I am afraid, was not included among the five best that we printed. It ran as follows:

I am a man approaching middle-age, but the only birthday I can distinguish among all the others was my twelfth. It was on that damp misty day in October that I met the Captain for the first time. I remember the wetness of the gravel in the school quad and the blown leaves which made the cloisters by the chapel slippery as I ran to escape from my enemies between one class and the next. I slithered and came to a halt and my pursuers went whistling away, for there in the middle of the quad stood our formidable headmaster talking to a tall man in a bowler hat who carried his walking stick over his shoulder at the slope like a rifle. I had no idea of course who he was or that he had won me the previous night at backgammon from my father.

As a parody, the real thing never works.
The entry became, eight years later, the opening passage of Greene's novel, *The Captain and the Enemy*

7 June 1980

At a medical college in Alexandria the students are actually taught that 90 per cent of British men are homosexuals. I hear this on good authority from a friend in Cairo, and I wonder how many other educational establishments in Egypt include this interesting item of information in their syllabuses. The answer could be the key to a curious experience I had in Aswan in Upper Egypt earlier this year. A Nubian boatman who was rowing me across the Nile decided to strike up a conversation. Having opened the batting with the usual Egyptian formalities – 'Welcome. You German? Germany good' – and having changed this, on learning of his mistake, to 'England good', he announced with great certainty: 'In England man marries man.' When I protested that, although the Church of England was

nowadays capable of practically anything, homosexual mar-
riages were still considered somewhat unusual, he insisted that
he was right, claiming that married homosexual couples were in
the habit of visiting Aswan. I wonder where these strange ideas
about British men have sprung from? There doesn't appear to
be any evidence that the British are more homosexually-
inclined than most other peoples, yet the whole world seems to
believe they are. And in Aswan, when I was there, the only
people who looked like homosexuals were French.

23 July 1983

Mr Auberon Waugh's capacity for stirring things up in the
sub-continent, while not yet on the scale of Mahatma Gandhi's,
is pretty impressive all the same. Some years ago he made some
comments about Islam in the *Times* which prompted a mob to
burn down the British Council Library in Rawalpindi. Just
lately he has caused an Indian member of Parliament to be
charged with a breach of parliamentary privilege. The MP, Mr
Kushwant Singh, writes a column in the *Hindustan Times*
under the appealing title 'With Malice Towards One and All'.
Perhaps unsurprisingly, Mr Waugh is his hero – 'my favourite
English political commentator'. In his column of 6 August Mr
Singh quoted extensively from an article by Mr Waugh in the
Spectator on the universally absorbing issue of MPs' pay. There
is a Bill before the Indian Parliament to double MPs' salaries
and fringe benefits, but, according to Mr Singh, Indian
newspapers, in contrast to the press in Britain, have not dared
to express any criticism – 'They are too scared of being hauled
up for contempt.' So instead of directly attacking his fellow

parliamentarians Mr Singh quoted Mr Waugh's view that 'most MPs are deeply unpleasant people, inspired by self-importance and greed to their calling and sustained in it by the lowest of motives throughout.' He concluded that for Indian MPs to vote themselves more money and privileges would be 'wrong and morally unjustifiable'. As a result, various notices of a breach of privilege were moved against Mr Singh in the Upper House of which he is a member. In his ruling on the matter, the Chairman of the Upper House, Mr Hidayatullah, described Mr Waugh's words as 'very sizzling' but concluded that Mr Singh had effectively protected himself against breach of privilege by quoting the opinions of somebody else.

10 September 1983

'As you prosper yourself, you ought to do something for others,' said Mrs Thatcher this week. It was an unexceptionable remark, but uttered on this occasion in a rather surprising context. The Prime Minister had just announced that she would be giving away single gloves from her wardrobe to one-handed people. There were two things which struck me as a bit odd about this. One was that Mrs Thatcher has ever lost a glove (she claimed to have 'one or two single gloves at home which I kept in the hope of finding the other'); the other was that she seemed to identify prosperity with possession of two hands and, by inference, the possession of only one hand with poverty. A single glove is in fact useless even to a pauper, if he happens to be a two-handed pauper. It is nevertheless an endearing scheme, organised by the Worshipful Company of Glovers of which Mrs Thatcher was made a member last Tuesday.

8 October 1983

Among the four South Korean cabinet ministers killed last Sunday by a bomb explosion in Rangoon was the country's Foreign Minister, Lee Bum-Suk. The newsreaders on television pronounced the name with great care as 'Boom-Sook', which most people will have assumed to be the correct Korean pronunciation. But this, I am sorry to say, is not the case. We telephoned the Korean embassy to find out more about the poor man, and a polite Korean diplomat with bad English pronounced it just as you or I would be tempted to. We were trying to find out whether Lee Bum-Suk was any relation of General Bum-Suk Lee who was Prime Minister of South Korea from 1948 to 1950. Apparently they are not related. Bum-Suk must be a common Korean name. Common or not, it is a name which in its prissier days the British press was embarrassed by. When General Bum-Suk Lee was Prime Minister, newspapers conspired not to refer to him by name at all. It fell to the late Peter Fleming in his 'Strix' column in the *Spectator* to draw attention to this omission. In our issue of 25 August, 1950 Mr Fleming wondered what had happened to the Korean Prime Minister. 'I know nothing of his attainments or capabilities, but his name is General Bum-Suk Lee and in some ways it seems rather a pity that he has disappeared from the news.'

15 October 1983

CHRISTOPHER FILDES

Late for a City date, I bounced into a taxi – and was startled to find that if offered, not only a telephone, but a list of excuses for being late. Pick up our telephone (suggested Racal, which supplies it) and tell them you are stuck behind the Lord Mayor's carriage. What happens, I asked the driver, if the Lord Mayor rings me back? I was reassured: the telephone only works outwards. This has very considerable scope. On my next journey, I shall ask the driver to call up some City worthy and say: 'Would you mind holding on for a moment – Mr Fildes is in his other taxi.'

3 May 1986

Progress report on the new scenic tramline, or Docklands Light Railway: its progress is fitful. The trams, like the rest of us, seem to be sensitive to the weather, and the automatic indicator boards are reduced to suggesting that passengers should look at the front of the trams. The contractors, riled by teasing comment, ring up to ask how they can be expected to sell their systems abroad. The response they get is predictable. It is now time to raise morale, as on British Railways, by giving the trams names (on handsome cast bronze nameplates) as well as numbers. *The Flying Docksman?* A class of local heroes – *Ben Tillett, Jack Dash, Reggie Kray, G. Ware Travelstead?* One for the great perpetual chairman of his city's Tramways and Fine Arts Committee, *Alderman Foodbotham?* I like the notices on the trams which show a thoughtful response to the line's floating population of journalists – urging: 'Please give up this seat to someone less able to stand than you.'

17 October 1987

Politicians in Washington and London must sympathise with the spokesman of the Republican Party, fighting a presidential election under difficulties, in 1932. He complained of a sinister conspiracy, rooted in Wall Street. Careful correlation had shown that, whenever the President made a statement designed to encourage confidence in the economy, the market invariably went down.

7 November 1987

"I suppose I'll have to put you down as loony right".

JOHN GRIGG

The authors of graffiti are humble artists, content that their work should swiftly perish. Of all forms of the art the most evanescent is the inscription made by a finger in dust or grime, which the first shower of rain is sure to wash away. I have just seen a white van, thickly coated with dirt, on whose side some passing wit has written, 'Also available in white.'

25 April 1987

RICHARD INGRAMS

We were talking over Sunday lunch about the funny things that happen to people on trains and John Piper came up with the following story. Some time about the beginning of the war the art critic Eric Newton was travelling in a compartment with a young girl who had with her a very large suitcase. At some time during the journey the girl took down the case and opened it. Newton was amazed to see that it was entirely filled with lemons – then impossible to buy in Britain. The girl offered him two which he accepted gratefully. No further conversation took place between the two of them but towards the end of the journey he presented his fellow traveller with one of his books that he happened to have with him, inscribing it: 'A poor exchange for two lemons. Eric Newton.' Some years passed and one day Newton received a letter out of the blue: 'Dear Mr Newton, You once inscribed a book to my daughter with the words "A poor exchange for two lemons". Would you kindly explain what you meant by this?' To which Newton replied: 'When I wrote "A poor exchange for two lemons", I meant exactly what I said.' He heard no more.

5 October 1985

I was privileged to be taken to lunch the other day at the Groucho Club, London's newest and most fashionable venue, where everyone spends half their time looking round to see who else is there. In this respect it is like the old Establishment Club from the dear dead days of the Sixties. Although the food is very good (but very expensive) I have no desire whatever to join. But then I have never felt the urge to belong to any club. Clubs, in my experience, are places where bores go to bore other people. Just belonging, they feel, entitles them to accost their fellow members and give them the benefit of their views. On a recent visit to the Garrick the three or four members I recognised were all people I would go out of my way to avoid. One of them, a prominent libel lawyer, was passing up and down the central table like an orderly officer in the army scattering his pearls hither and thither. I buried my face in the Brown Windsor. At the Coach and Horses, a venue familiar to Jeffrey Bernard's readers and the nearest place to a club that I frequent, you can actually be thrown out for being a bore. I have seen with my own eyes an unfortunate American publisher called Jay Landesman being told to leave by Norman when half way through his lunch. 'But why?' he stammered, his fork raised to his lips. 'Because you're such a f—— bore,' said Norman calmly removing his plate. Funnily enough, who should I see on my recent visit, propping up the bar at the Groucho, but Mr Landesman? Looking serene and at ease, he had found a safe refuge at last.

12 October 1985

CHARLES MOORE

Nouvelle cuisine may well have introduced some exciting new tastes and textures but it has also imposed some strange rules. The necessity of kiwi fruit with everything ('What are these funny cucumbers?', I remember Roy Kerridge asking once) has been pointed out; so has the determination to make radishes into little flowers. But there is an even stricter doctrine about vegetables, which I encountered again the other day. A friend took me to a restaurant and I asked for beans with the main dish. This was not possible. All that was served was 'a selection of fresh vegetables', which would contain the odd bean, but to

supply a plate with nothing but beans would destroy the finely balanced eco-system which flourished behind the swing-doors of the kitchen. Eventually they compromised, and I was allowed beans alone, but not very many of them. Suppose one asked for lamb, and was presented with 'a selection of fresh meats'.

10 May 1986

KEITH WATERHOUSE

I had occasion to get in a case of champagne last week. The wine store where I buy the occasional bottle having a sign in its window promising a delivery service, I asked them to send one round. Of course, it didn't arrive. When I rang to ask where the wine was, this was the conversation:

'Oh, no, I'm afraid there's been a misunderstanding – we don't do deliveries of less than half a dozen cases.'

'Then why did your man accept my order for one?'

'I don't know, but he shouldn't have done.'

'Whether he should have done or not, he did, and I've been waiting in the whole morning.'

'All right, then, as a favour we'll send a case round.'

'I don't want it as a favour, thank you. This is a perfectly straightforward commercial transaction.'

'Not from our point of view – there's very little profit in our house champagne.'

My option at this point was either to accept the 'favour' with ill grace, or to decline it with even worse grace. My need, or rather that of my impending guests, being great, I gave in, reflecting as I did so that if I were in New York I could have had a bottle of Coca-Cola sent round with less of a song and dance. What a country this is to try to buy things in. I think that someone ought to keep a disgruntled consumer's diary, then publish it as the belated reverse side to Fothergill's *Diary of an Innkeeper*.

17 January 1987

ALAN WATKINS

I must tell the story of the daughter of a friend who found a job as secretary to a couple of 'executives' on the *Daily Mirror*. Asked about her duties, she replied: 'I have to get them bacon sandwiches when they come back to the office hungry after lunch.'

1 October 1984

Reading the autobiographies of Mr John Mortimer, Mr Eric Newby and Sir Woodrow Wyatt, I was struck by one thing they had in common. Their fathers, respectively a barrister, a businessman and a preparatory school headmaster, seemed to spend most of their waking hours in a simply terrible temper. 'Confound you, Sir, why can't you look where you're going?' or similar sentiments seem to have been expressed virtually hourly. A friend of mine says this disposition must have been brought about by constipation, endemic in the early years of this century. I favour a more Marxist explanation: Englishmen of that class and generation felt sufficiently powerful and secure to be as rude as they pleased.

3 May 1986

The 'Media Correspondent' of *The Times* writes in relation to the Tate Gallery extension: 'Turner, the diminutive romantic artist born in London in 1775, has always been capable of generating controversy.' This is almost though not quite as good as what a *Mirror* soccer correspondent once wrote about a new young Israeli player: 'Israel, the country that gave us the fabulous Jesus Christ, has produced yet another boy wonder.'

4 April 1987

RICHARD WEST

Brighton

'He eats more oysters than the Dukes' was the saying attributed to a waiter at the Beefsteak club with reference to Paul Johnson, who this week addressed a Conservative meeting at Brighton. Such jokes were of course more piquant when Paul was a socialist and editor of the *New Statesman*. I can remember once in an editorial conference how he was holding forth on some Labour measure – the Industrial Relations Act, I think – and clinched his argument by saying that 'Everybody I meet is in favour of it . . . for instance the Duke of Devonshire told me yesterday . . .' There was a splendid misunderstanding, also in conference at the *New Statesman*, when Paul and an earnest, bearded contributor spent several minutes discussing the Marquess of Anglesey, with Paul referring to his friend the nobleman, and the ebc referring to a pub of the same name.

14 October 1978

A. N. WILSON

A neighbour of mine, a polite man of charming manners, has a horror of beards. If possible, he refuses Beavers entry into his house. He even went so far as to post an invitation to a family newly arrived in the district (whom he had not met), but to cancel the party when the unfortunate Dad arrived on the scene sprouting facial hair. It is an odd obsession. My own father used to have a touch of it, and described how as a child during the reign of the bearded Edward VII he would be tempted to shout 'Beaver!' at bearded passers by. Now he has an elegant beard himself, rather like that of Cardinal Mazarin. The most surprising people do dislike beards. I would always have assumed, for instance, that Iris Murdoch had moved in a very Bohemian world where, even during the 1950s and 1960s, beards were common, but she once told me that she disliked beards very much because they spoil the beauty of a man's face. I suppose the argument in favour of beards gains strength when the man's face isn't all that beautiful. I wonder if I shall ever become beard-obsessed? I felt a flicker of the sensation the other day on a Number 7 bus going up Oxford Street. I was the only person on the top floor, including the conductor, who was not draped with cheek-fungus. I am illogical on the subject. I like the sight of a long flowing beard, such as might be seen on a Greek Orthodox archimandrite, or a rabbi, but I dislike the very short stubbly beards which some people have nowadays. This is to ignore the fact that great oaks from little acorns grow.

7 April 1984

PEREGRINE WORSTHORNE

Has anybody else noticed how the young nowadays sit down in bus queues, instead of standing? I suppose they don't mind dirtying their jeans. One little group in Fulham, in expectation of the long wait for a Number 11, had brought a thermos of tea, intended more to assuage impatience than thirst. They offered me a cup, and I sat down too, feeling a bit foolish. But in fact it was an excellent idea for passing the time, at least in the summer.

9 July 1977

CYRIL RAY

PRE-WOLFENDEN

The call-girl system will boom, we are told, if the Wolfenden
recommendations sweep clean the streets: has any constructive
thought been given to the consequent strain on the space
available for small advertisements in the newsagents' windows
of Soho and Shepherd Market – 'French Lessons by Miss Flogg:
42, 24, 36?'

Let me commend to some enterprising publisher the notion
of reviving *The Man of Pleasure's Illustrated Pocket-Book*, an
annual vade-mecum, the 1850 issue of which I keep in my study
– in a locked drawer – to dip into whenever I have had a smug
sufficiency of the more stern and unbending writers of the
period. (Only Surtees needs no corrective.) Its title-page
proclaims its function: 'displaying at one glance the varied
attractions of this great metropolis; with correct details of the
saloons, clubs and night houses, ball concert and billiard
rooms, casinos, comical clubs, theatres, introducing houses
. . . rendering it a Complete and Gentlemanly Night Guide,'
and the other end of the small, leather-bound volume, where
there is a gusset for a pencil, forms a pocket for 'cards of address
of a select few attractive lasses of this our "little village."'

The good Queen had been on the throne for thirteen years,
and married for most of them to Albert, also the Good; but
there was still a dog-fighting and rat-killing house in Bunhill
Row, where the visitor 'will find a night not ill spent, at least if
he has spirit enough to be interested in a display of good old
English "pluck" both in men and dogs. Admission to the killing
matches, 1s.'

At Jessop's, in the Strand, could be found, according to the
Guide, 'all the most nobby ladies in town . . . and also some of
the right sort of swells.' No doubt this was a cut above similar
establishments on the other side of the water, where the Surrey
Saloon, for instance, was kept by 'George Nash, a dashing

blade', and 'frequented by the better sort of girls on the Surrey side of the metropolis' – though 'Mary Weeland, alias the Snowdrop, a frequenter of the Surrey' often slipped away to the wine-and-supper rooms opposite Astley's – 'a prime piece of luscious loveliness and whose astringent qualities have given all pleasure that have got her good graces.' Astringent?

Tiresome of the Snowdrop to be now at this address, now at that; but there were ladies of the town who were more constant in their professional inconstancy. Under the general, poetic heading of 'Paphian Bowers' are listed some score of names and addresses, provocatively 'enriched with engravings', ranging from those of Miss Fowler, Church Street, Soho (who 'previous to the first *faux pas* which led to the present state of her affairs, exhibited her beautiful person in famed Cranbourne Alley, known by the appellation of the Fairy Queen . . . She is a bewitching girl; is to be met with at her residence here described, and is to be had by bidding for'), to Miss A. Parks, Beaufort Place, New Road (*'the house will be known by the Venetian blinds generally drawn down'*): 'She makes no scruple of getting as much as she possibly can from her foreign visitors, but will not refuse five pounds from a British hand.'

Is there a touch – the merest touch – of Victorian hypocrisy about the tribute to Miss Jane Wilmott, of York Place, Knightsbridge: *name on brass plate* ('She is seldom guilty of those vices which we so frequently censure, and which defile the sex more than any other: we mean drinking and swearing')? Mme. Lemiercier's Wandsworth Road establishment is 'to be found by a brazen plate on the door, signifying, "A Seminary for Young Ladies." This we dub the artful dodge.' As for Madame Maurin's stay- and corset-making house in Waterloo Road, 'this caper is about the neatest stitch we have tumbled to . . . everything is kept very dark here, and snug's the word. No cully is admitted here before daylight has mizzled, and then he must *hook it* before "daylight does appear," and then scarper by the back door.'

In case the vocabulary should perturb the intending client, a glossary, 'The Modern Flash Dictionary', is appended, including many terms that have since risen to relative respectability –diddle, rumpus, sidle, yoke – and many more which have not. Some of the words have passed out of currency – to the language's loss?

Angelicas: Young, unmarried ladies.
Dimber mot: An enchanting girl.
Fogle: Handkerchief.
Snuge: Thief under bed.
Cucumbers: Tailors.
Scandal broth: Tea.
Wooden ruff: Pillory.

Bibliographers tell me that these annual volumes, although they were published in fairly large editions, substantially bound, and so relatively recently, are pretty rare: outraged Victorian widows, finding them among their deceased husbands' effects, would fling them indignantly on the fire. Not that the publisher, the helpful and well-meaning Mr Ward, would have wished his Gentlemanly Night Guide to fall into the hands of married men. So I assume from the fact that his office in the Strand, when not described as 'Ward's Sporting and Parisian Repository', was austerely advertised as a 'Bachelor's Repository of the Arts'. This we dub the artful dodge.

27 September 1957

ALAN RUSBRIDGER

A VINTAGE VISCOUNT

John Clotworthy Talbot Foster Whyte-Melville Skeffington, the 13th Viscount Massereene and Ferrard, was not quite himself on Thursday 3 March, as you might perhaps guess from the following abrupt exchange:

> *Viscount Massereene and Ferrard*: The noble Lord is out of order; this is the Report stage of the Bill.
> *Lord Bellwin*: No, this is the committee stage.
> *Viscount Massereene and Ferrard*: Yes, so it is; I am sorry.

A little later, the Viscount got into something of a muddle in the course of suggesting that the unemployed should receive petrol vouchers for travelling to job interviews. Lord Sefton of Garston was moved to comment: 'Someone suggested to me once that the House of Lords is not of this world. That speech has just demonstrated it.'

In the context of the Upper House, this is blood all over the walls. It is superfluous to say that the House of Lords is a gentlemanly place, but it is a rare thing for even the most senile, rambling peer to attract any form of interruption, let alone the sort of rebuff meted out by Lord Sefton of Garston. Whoever imagined that Viscount Massereene and Ferrard was out of this world anyway? His admirers know him to be of quite a different world. In a sentence, and to borrow one of the Viscount's own striking images, he belongs to a world in which one could safely leave an unlocked parked car in the centre of London with suitcases in it.

But, straight away, let us get a flavour of Massereene and Ferrard on a good day, for otherwise it will be difficult to appreciate the concern that one feels on reading of Lord Sefton of Garston's outburst. The following contribution to the committee stage of the Wildlife and Countryside Bill in 1981 is quintessential Massereene and Ferrard. He is talking of bulls:

'The only annoying thing which happened to me – cattle are very inquisitive – was when one shorthorn of mine went to investigate a hiker's tent. They were not there, and he got tangled up in the guy ropes, and somehow unfortunately got a frying pan attached to his horn. This was extremely annoying for the cows, because whenever he tried to get near them they heard this thing banging and fled. It was also very annoying for me, becuase I could not get a cow served, and in the end the poor bull had to be shot.

'I have had some extremely endearing bulls. I had one Ayrshire bull down in Kent who was extremely friendly. One day he walked into a wedding reception in the village hall. He was, of course, perfectly harmless but caused a bit of a panic. I believe he also knocked over the wedding cake.'

Vintage. Indeed, the passage of the Wildlife and Countryside Bill through the Lords in the spring of 1981 was a vintage period altogether for Massereene and Ferrard and he spoke no fewer than 77 times. Again he is talking of bulls: 'It is no good putting up notices saying "Beware of the Bull" because very rude things are sometimes written on them. I have found that one of the most effective notices is "Beware of the Agapanthus".' And here he is talking of catapults: 'The only time I fired a catapult as a boy was at a sparrow in London. I got into awful trouble. It went through somebody's bathroom window and hit an old man on the head while he was in the bath. My father got the blame.'

The anecdotal tone is the hallmark. There are few subjects to which the lordships turn their minds during the course of any year upon which Massereene and Ferrard will not feel himself qualified to speak, and few that he will be unable to embellish with a short narrative drawn from his own experience.

Not the more eye-catching experiences, mind you. He is tantalisingly brief on how he came to drive the leading British car in the 1937 Le Mans Grand Prix or how he came to be presenting *Countess Maritza* at the Palace Theatre. But it is seldom that he will touch on trade union legislation or the decline of British industry without referring to the time he once owned a small factory. It was a plastics factory in Deal and he is fond of telling how he acquired it sort of by mistake. Then, another day, he will announce that he once had an interest in tramp steamers. Again, he will begin a deer debate with the statement: 'My lords, I think I should begin by declaring my interest, which is probably fairly well known. I own a deer forest.'

It must then have been with a certain keenness of anticipation that their lordships awaited Massereene and Ferrard's contribution to the debate on the Brixton disturbances. He did not disappoint them. 'My Lords,' he began, 'I think I am the only Member who has spoken today who had agricultural estates in Jamaica.' Pure finesse. He kept it up: 'I went there regularly for 12 years after the war, and so I got to know the people extremely well. In all the time I went out there I never came across any riots. The only riots I ever came across were riots of joy on the estate, because when I arrived I always gave a big barbeque for all the children and the people and it was a riot of joy.'

You believe him. It would be. Sadly, not all his experiences with black people have been so happy: 'I recall that when independence was coming certain things happened: for example, on one occasion when I was parking my car in Kingston – actually my estate was on the west coast of Jamaica, whereas Kingston is on the east coast – I asked a black man if he would mind backing his car a few feet to enable me to park mine, and he said; "You want me to do that only because you are white and I am black." I replied: "Don't be so silly. Nothing of the sort. If you don't want to move I will find somewhere else to park." But once that sort of attitude crept in I felt it was time to leave.'

There is something of the Don't Be So Silly in most of what Massereene and Ferrard has to say on any given topic. He is a fervent believer in common sense, a commodity which, to his never-ceasing despair and wonder, he finds to be in remarkably short supply – even, it has to be said, amongst his fellow peers. There is no disingenuousness or irony about the frequent preface: 'I am a simple man.'

Prisons, for instance. 'Would not the commonsense method to do away with overcrowding in prisons be to build more prisons?' he asks. 'It would also provide more employment. It seems to me a very simple problem.' Or (from June 1979)

British Rail: 'If you travel by British Rail you find the trains are often late. And what is the usual excuse? The usual excuse is shortage of staff. God Almighty! When there are nearly one and a half million people unemployed what is the excuse for shortage of staff? It does not add up.'

To the 68-year-old Massereene and Ferrard there are more and more things about the world today that do not add up, and he does not mind admitting it. Each speech is an enchanting mixture of dogmatism and bewilderment. 'I am rather ignorant on this matter ... It is not quite my line of country ... Perhaps I am missing the point ... I may not have read the Bill properly.'

For the plain fact of the matter is ... well, Massereene and Ferrard put the plain fact of the matter himself in the foreword to his book on the House of Lords in 1973: 'I have witnessed the swift disintegration of everything the word "British" once stood for and I have seen the world, in consequence, become a poorer place.' You see? Massereene and Ferrard is not of this world: he is a throwback to another world; the world, for shorthand's sake, of Sir Richard Hannay and Sir Edward Leithen.

'We are on a 100 per cent wicket here ... I shall change the bowling for three or four minutes and speak on ... I will now change horses and speak for a few minutes on ...' He certainly speaks like a Buchan hero: 'It always amazes me that so many people actually think that 56 million of us can live in this country by hanging out each other's washing.' And, of course, almost every detail of his life fits: Eton, Black Watch, Monday Club, Scottish estates, field sports, Carlton, Turf, Pratt's, Royal Yacht Squadron. (His coat of arms, appropriately enough, sports two stags, no fewer than six bulls and, inappropriately enough, a mermaid combing her hair in a mirror.) He is popular, he is charming, and by way of a final, endearing idiosyncrasy, he has a stammer which in his public speaking he has learned to cope with by the liberal use of the word 'actually'. His record, so far as anyone knows, is 211 in one speech. (It is impossible to be certain about this, for Hansard writers are under standing orders to excise the word from the official record.)

And yet he is attacked by Lord Sefton of Garston. One might

choose to ignore Lord Sefton of Garston's attack were it not for the fact that it is but one recent instance of Massereene and Ferrard's colleagues in the Upper House indulging in public displays of impatience with his contributions. Only last year Lord Molloy, in an outburst of passion rare in the second chamber, accused Massereene and Ferrard of 'jumping up and making silly statements'.

Over the years, it must be said, the Lords and Ladies who grace Parliament have seldom shown signs of taking Viscount Massereene and Ferrard's speeches over-seriously. But that an increasing number of peers should begin to greet them with ill-concealed sarcasm and plain ill manners is a disturbing trend. They should realise that Viscount Massereene and Ferrard, to a greater extent than many of them, is an endangered species and that his admirers – an esoteric, but growing band – will be monitoring future developments carefully before deciding whether more urgent measures are needed to protect that species. As a first step, an approach will be made to the Lord Chancellor, Lord Hailsham, whose preface to Massereene and Ferrard's book on the House of Lords stated, more eloquently than we could hope to do, what many of us feel: 'One hopes that Viscount Massereene and Ferrard will never be reformed.'

26 March 1983

"You can die naturally, or of course we can do it for you".

MURRAY SAYLE

SO AT THAT POINT I . . .

An acceptance, last week, to mourn the passing of General Moshe Dayan prevented my celebrating an altogether happier occasion, namely the 100th anniversary of the famous newspaper, the *Sunday People*. The editor of the *Spectator* was, I can now disclose, less than enthusiastic – sniffy, even – about the project, possibly because our distinguished contemporary outsells his magazine by close to 200 to one. 'I'll bet *The People* doesn't advertise in our 8,000th number, which is just coming up,' he said. 'Anyway, we are 154 years old next July, even in our present series, so what are they on about? We'd only make them look important.' To which,

I replied

Sir: I beg to differ, and crave space in your valued publication to put the record straight. In the first place, I consider *The People* has set an admirable standard, over the years, of popular journalism, even without the benefit of Australian ownership. Further, the expressions 'We Name the Guilty Men' and 'At that point, I made an excuse and left' first appeared in its pages, a fact which must interest any lover of the English language.

What's more, I am very likely the last person alive who actually made such an excuse, left, and am still here to tell the tale.

Respectfully, etc.,

Murray Sayle
onetime
Junior Reporter and
Assistant Vice Exposer,
The People,
Old Grub Street
London EC4.

Oh, very well, if you have to. But try to keep it short. Ed.

So, fade out on today's confident present, and flash back to December 1952, the year I arrived, hot from the Sydney *Daily Mirror*, the traditional fiver in my pocket, determined to break into the business in the Old Country. London was caught in the last of the great Six Day Killer Smogs, and Britain gave a first, indelible impression of a nation stumbling along in the dark, uncertain where it was going. Every day, in a bus led along like some blinded elephant by a conductor tapping the footpath, a packet of ten Weights in my pocket, I made my way from my modest digs in the Earl's Court Road to Fleet Street, looking for a job.

In view of its record on appeasement, I naturally drew the line at the *Times*, and the *Sunday Times* in those days already had a reporter. However, strolling through the zoo, as it were, of Fleet Street, my eye was caught by *The People* (as we shall henceforth call it; everyone knows it comes out on Sundays). The name had a pleasant leftish sound and, as the curse of social class was about to disappear, I'd be in on the ground floor of the New Elizabethan age, where talent alone counted. So, I wrote off, stating that I was well-travelled (how had I got to Earl's Court?) and spoke fluent Urdu (our ship had called at Bombay). I was not surprised to get a letter back proposing an interview the following Tuesday.

In those days *The People* offices were in Covent Garden, at the top of Bow Street, both places I had heard of. I couldn't say the same for my interviewer, one Renton Stuart Campbell, the managing editor, known as 'Sam'. Campbell seemed unimpressed by the literary skill and political acumen which I felt I could bring to his paper, or even the fact that I once had my by-line drawn in twigs on the gardening page of the Sydney *Daily Telegraph*. But he seemed to like my accent, and said 'Ye look tough enough for the job, laddie. We'll give ye a week's trial. Come and meet Tommy Webb.' I was thereupon introduced to Duncan Webb, *The People*'s crime man. I had encountered, I soon discovered, one of the most famous double acts in all journalism.

Over brown ale (we are in pre-Thomson days, no brandy lunches then) Webb outlined the assignment. Under Campbell's direction, he explained, he was about to break one of the hottest stories even the old Street had ever seen. Most of the London vice world, it seemed, was controlled by five evil Maltese brothers, named Messina. Piece by piece, he had uncovered a web (writing it up later, we made that 'network') of corruption and villainy stretching through the very heart of the capital and, at that time, Empire. Webb's methods were simple, painstaking, and effective. After establishing that premises were being used for the purposes of prostitution, as defined by Stone's *Justices' Manual*, he would track back the ownership of the property, through as many as half-a-dozen front men and flimsy companies, to the Messinas. Confrontations would then follow, sometimes accompanied by punch-ups and death threats. The Messinas, he mentioned off-handedly, had body-guards who carried two-foot-long stilettos, unlike the bicycle chains and brass knuckles used by decent British villains.

The problem was, said Webb, that the Messinas had rumbled him – not surprisingly, as his picture appeared in *The People* every week, where he was accurately described as Fleet Street's top crime reporter. His picture was now posted in every house of ill repute in London. To complete his exposure, more evidence was wanted. 'I need someone who couldn't be me, and couldn't be a copper,' he explained. 'As a big wool man straight off the boat, looking for a bit of the old you-know-what, you'd be perfectly convincing, digger.'

How, I asked, do we establish that the premises are being used for prostitution? Apart from the obvious way? The sword of reform, I assumed, would have to be raised shining and untarnished. 'You have to get a definite offer of sex,' said Webb. 'Get them to disrobe and name a price. Like, how much for a short time, and how much for an all-nighter. Don't actually hand over any cash, though. Sam would never stand for throwing the firm's money around like that.'

'And then?'

'You make some sort of excuse, and leave. And make sure you do leave.'

'Oh.'

My first assignment was in Shepherds Market. Webb waited in a nearby ABC Tearooms while I climbed a winding stair and knocked, as firmly as I could manage, on a door marked 'French lessons'. 'Come in,' said a bored, another-day-another-dollar voice.

Now, while I knew in a general way from Eng. Lit. II that,

> The harlot's cry from street to street
> Shall weave old England's winding sheet

I had not, up to that point, actually met one of these ladies in the flesh, especially one that talked like a pre-Higgins Eliza Doolittle. She was youngish, hair in curlers, sprawled on a bed reading a women's magazine. Fanciable, actually, in circumstances less *folklorique*.

'Bonjour,' I tried.

'Sorry, love,' she said. 'No foreigners.'

'I'm a wool man, straight off the boat,' I reassured her. There was a long pause. Then I said, 'Er, how much?'

'For what, dear?'

'How much a short time, and how much an all-nighter?' While, of course, people do perform the *danse de Trèves* in Australia, these particular terms are not currently in use, and I may have sounded unconvincing.

'It depends,' she said wearily, 'on whether you're a regular or not.'

'How do you become a regular?'

'By coming here regularly, of course. 'She used a pitying tone, as to someone a strawberry or two short of the punnet.

'You don't . . . ,' I said, 'you don't feel like, er, disrobing, do you?'

'Look dear, if you're one of those sex perverts, like, I don't do that sort of kinky stuff,' she said.

Conversation seemed to have dried up. 'I just remembered,' I said, 'I left my wallet at home. Back in a flash.' And left.

Webb was not pleased with my bumbling performance, but patient with a beginner. 'Let's do the next one together,' he suggested, 'and I'll show you the form.' The next place was altogether grander, a mansion in SW1. The lady in charge, Webb said, had a son at Eton. But somewhere in the background lurked the Messinas.

'We're doing a course at Portsmouth,' Webb explained. 'Freshening up on torpedoes.' A genial Irishman who went in for crested blazers with handkerchiefs tucked up the sleeve, Webb did indeed have a weatherbeaten, naval look about him. 'My clobber here is R.A.N,' he added.

'We don't do, er, groups, actually,' said the lady in charge. 'But you have adjoining rooms, if you like.'

I went upstairs with a young lady more the Vivien Leigh type. We sat on a sofa. 'What's a nice girl. . . .' I began, but abandoned this approach as being a trifle *vieux jeu*. We got on to her political views, which seemed to be Conservative. 'What's the system of payment here?' I asked, to get the conversation around to the business of the day. 'Downstairs,' she replied. 'We just work here.' What was she, hard-up governess, bored housewife, lady novelist in search of material? I was about to suggest a meeting outside somewhere to discuss her real feelings about life, something along the lines of *Waterloo Bridge*, when the door was wrenched open and Webb burst in.

'Let's get out of here, digger,' he shouted dramatically. 'These women are not clean.' There goes *Waterloo Bridge*, I thought. 'It's the war,' I improvised wildly, as we left, over my shoulder. 'Malaria. He gets these queer turns now and again. Sorry.' Webb slammed the front door, decorated with a handsome pair of antique bronze knockers, as we left.

'Look Tom, we may have hurt those girls' feelings,' I said.

'That's the secret of a good excuse,' Webb explained. 'That stuff about "I just remembered something I have to do" just makes them suspicious. A good excuse should have surprise value, the sort of thing a real client might say.'

Webb and I, in the weeks that followed, developed a working relationship with much of the quiet comradeship of a fishing trip in good company. We sat outside brothels in a *People* car, clocking clients in and out while we discussed the ultimate questions of love, life and the modern novel. Webb, a man of religious convictions, felt nothing but compassion for the Magdalenes offering themselves for hire, and corresponding distaste for the Messinas who, it seemed, were getting the lions' share of the take. Looking back, I can see that our attitudes in those days were possibly tinged with racism, or at least anti-Latin and -Arab prejudice (if this is, indeed what Maltese are). Had the brothers been Norwegian, for instance, concealing their activities behind a chain of Scandinavian open-faced sandwich shops, they might well have been hailed as prophets of the oncoming new permissiveness. But, *autre temps* . . .

Tirelessly following up leads like 'Young Lady has Opening for Active Handy Man', BIG CHEST FOR SALE, and 'Chairs Recaned and Rebottomed, Satisfaction Guaranteed', we steadily built up a picture of the Messinas' activity. The series, launched under the headline, WE NAME THE GUILTY MEN, accompanied by a row of mugshots of the brothers, scarred and scowling under snap-brim hats, duly created a national sensation. Even their white Rolls-Royces, which these days would at least show that the family were buying British, then seemed to make their life-style even more offensive, sullying as it did the colour of Royal weddings and untouched virginity.

The Messinas were denounced in the House of Lords and run out of town, only filtering back, gradually, when the heat was off. Webb went on to exploits in their way even more remarkable. He starred, for instance, in the first television commercials ever made for a newspaper in Britain (for *The People*, naturally), pipe stuck in his mouth, Irish jaw jutting behind his battered Imperial Upright, typing up another definitive list of Guilty Men.

He was brutally beaten with knuckle-dusters by a gangster named Jack Spot, not, as it turned out, for threatening to expose him, but in a literary discussion over the first British Serial rights of Spot's confessions, *I Am The King of London's Underworld*, which Webb had ghostwritten in his usual workmanlike style. Sent with £50,000 of *People* money to buy the confessions of Burgess and Maclean, said by a party of Yugoslav fishermen to be holed up on a remote island in the Adriatic, Webb discovered that he would be sailing alone with the fishermen and prudently bought a 9mm Beretta Banker's Special to protect the firm's cash. Needless to say, B&M never appeared, and Webb returned to the office with the funds and the gun, for which he naturally claimed on his expenses. Campbell, a man with a Murdochian eye for an expense sheet, directed his secretary to 'tell Webb to take the gun down to Soho and sell it. We're nae buying him any free toys.' Astonished reporters in the *People* newsroom saw Webb, his expense claim in one hand and a pistol in the other, enter Campbell's office to expostulate with him, and return with his expenses signed, thus becoming immortal in Fleet Street (if he wasn't already) as the only reporter ever to collect his expenses at the point of a gun.

Webb died, tragically young, in the late Fifties. He did not, as the Fleet Street joke has it, make an excuse first, having in my opinion nothing in his career that needed excusing. Quite to the contrary, Webb set a standard of honest reporting later to flower in the various Insights, Daylights and other forms of group-grope investigative journalism which have since chewed up so many Finnish forests. But no one ever did it better, or produced a worse set of bad guys than the Messinas (who would probably be well on their way to the peerage now, in our days of mass-marketed naughtiness). A standard, I might add, well maintained by *The People* and its reporters in the years that followed. But space is running out, and I am, perhaps, going on a bit. And I suddenly remember something I have to do down in the Earl's Court Road. So at this point I. . . .

31 October 1981

NORMAN STONE

AN ENGLISHMAN IN OLD POLAND

One curiosity about living in Oxfordshire, as I do, is that you come across, quite often, the relics of empire. Its servants like to retire to the country, where their descendants stayed on, together with family papers. I was recently shown a splendidly bound volume of letters, sent back from Warsaw in 1919–1920, by a British colonel, John Seymour Mellor, who was sent out to advise the Poles as to how they should establish a police force. The result is a good little period piece.

The letters run from October 1919 to May 1920. It was a time of great chaos in Warsaw. The new Polish state had only just come into existence; its borders were fought over, the currency was in a mess, the country had been ravaged by the First World War, and Poles of the various parts under different rulers were widely different in character. The national hero, Marshal Pilsudski, was head of state, and commanded the loyalty of an army that dressed in several different uniforms: the Church was strong; a figure of international prestige, Paderewski, the pianist, had volunteered to be President. In an effort to create a proper state, the police were to be organised with British help, and Mellor, a well-connected staff officer with experience of organising the occupied part of Germany, was sent out with a small team (paid, in hard currency, by the Poles).

The first letter describes a journey through Paris – desperately expensive – via Switzerland and poverty-stricken Vienna to the Czechoslovak border. Here, 'a rude official attempted to turn us out of the train as we had not a visé [sic] for his rotten country . . . We were firm and told him that there were now so many small states to think of that this had been forgotten when visés were obtained.' Then comes Warsaw, an office in the Ministry of the Interior, and rooms at the Hotel Bristol (which had been built by Paderewski on the edge of the Old Town, before the First World War. The Germans used it during the Second World War, and it therefore survived their destruction of Warsaw: and it is now – taking years and years – being restored). It does not cost very much – a huge lunch for two for 10/- at the Europejski Hotel near the Bristol (it, too, is still going strong in Thirties style). First impressions: 'all the people we have to deal with are very nice'. Connections are excellent. There are some very good Englishmen around – General Carton de Wiart, a sort of Ritchie-Hook who was much loved in Poland, and witnessed the campaign of 1939; 'Cavendish-Bentinck', the then third secretary, later, in 1945, British ambassador and now, at a great age, the Duke of Portland; the consul, Professor Savory, also in later years a good friend to the Poles. Cards are then left with various Poles, particularly Count Adam Zamoyski, a friend of friends.

The Western visitor to Poland was, is and will be struck by a sense of surrealism. This is partly because of the national habit of drinking far, far too much. The colonel has to get used to endless toasts of 'short drinks' and reckons, at the end, that he could drink a barrel of vodka without blinking – which I doubt. A Count 'Petoski' (Potocki) has parties which go on more or less every day until 4 a.m. and lunches at the Europesjki last from 1.15 to 3.45. Besides, 'the language seems hopeless. It is impossible to catch the words.' At a Zamoyski party, 'Everyone was a prince or princess or count and of course with impossible names which we were quite unable to catch. It is a most difficult business, this name problem, for one is supposed to call on the people one sits next to during the following 48 hours.' In fact, if they are ladies, then you have to leave cards the very next day, and this is very difficult because (no doubt with a terrible hangover) you don't know the names and can't pronounce the street-names while your drozhky driver cannot read. Count 'Petoski', who was once ADC to the Tsar, is helpful; so is Count Adam, though the colonel is disconcerted when, at 12.45 a.m., he calls in the hotel room to hand over a dinner invitation for the same day. Social life is overwhelmingly aristocratic – inevitably, in view of language problems – and there is the usual international bubble-existence, then starting up seriously for the first time in history: parties after the opera with a Russian colonel of the Red Cross, a French staff colonel, a Romanian, Major Pallavicino from Italy whose children speak

six languages: Belgians staging a lavish national day in the midst
of starvation: 'a woman in rags came through the swing doors
and went up to the centre of the room and suddenly fell flat on
the floor. No one paid any attention,' until an American got hot
milk for her.

The aristocracy are undoubtedly patriotic, though rather in
the spirit expressed by a Count Ronikier to the German
ambassador in Vienna: 'If Poland could be free and independent, I'd give half of my worldly goods. With the other half, I'd
emigrate.' In the first place, the new Poland is rather Left-
inclined, and requisitions the nobles' palaces (which anyway
consist of huge public rooms, with a warren of tiny bedrooms;
and all other places in Warsaw consist of flats). Some of the
nobles have seen the Russian Revolution, and lost everything: a
Princess Pignatelli – the name, though Italian, is Polish-Russian
aristocratic, but the lady is English and lives in France: a sort of
wagon-lit nobility – is extraordinarily long-winded and boring
on the subject, though Prince Mirsky (who ended up writing a
biography of Lenin, being converted to Bolshevism, going back
and being killed by Stalin) has them all 'in roars of laughter'.
There is Dzierzynski, cousin of the founder of Lenin's secret
police, whose house was burned down; a British officer from
Russia shows photographs of Bolshevik atrocities, 'heaps of
bodies of people buried alive with their legs and hands tied up
. . . others who had had their arms and feet cut off, others who
had been beaten to death with sticks'.

On the other hand, 'no wonder Bolshevism thrives in such
countries': there is a degree of heartlessness among the better-
off – though Prince Janusz Radziwill runs his estate, 60 miles
from Warsaw, with conspicuous fairness and efficiency. But,
more particularly, administration, police and rationing are all in
terrible disarray; there is one strike after another, and the
currency dwindles in value from week to week. 'I am sorry for
the country, as I like the Pole, but he is hopeless at present.'
When, for instance, the Poles took over Poznan from the
Germans, the ceremony did not take place at the appointed
hour because the Poles, having failed to adjust their watches to
Central European time, were an hour late: there was a fight,
with some deaths, in consequence; later, when Pilsudski
arrived as head of state, his carriage was unhooked by mistake

"Looks like you've hit the jackpot ol' son".

and he sat fuming outside the town, and missed the ceremonies. Elsewhere, a stadium is built for a parade, and then no tickets are issued for it, so that it is not used and *prominenti* mill around: at another time, tickets are issued, but then someone forgets to built a stadium. 'My opinion of the Polish administration is such that I wonder at nothing they do. They are hopeless.'

The government is out of a fable. Decent old Paderewski goes on and on, at private dinner parties, about the Yellow Peril (not the Red one, which is closer) and his wife dominates everything, to the extent of keeping (and forgetting) State telegrams in her handbag. Marshal Pilsudski is a good egg, with sufficient sense of irony to laugh at himself, the one-time socialist, being taken round an exhibition of Italian art by an excruciating professor, and with a retinue of Czartoryskis and Tyszkiewiczes. The national anthem takes ten minutes to play: religious ceremonies go on and on and on. Parliament has a left-wing majority: 'no collars and no ties; dirty; ill-behaved and very obviously uneducated'; one visit to this distinguished assembly would impress upon one for life the necessity of doing one's utmost to prevent socialists getting into Parliament.'

Outside the formerly Prussian and Austrian parts which show 'what education can do', Poland reflects the ills of Tsarist Russia. As you go from 'Lakapania' (Zakopane) over the old border to Lublin, you are into poor houses, poor agriculture, drunkenness, illiteracy: 'the villages very dirty and full of filthy dirty Jews' who manage all the trade and occupy a rabbit-warren-like part of Warsaw. 'The Jew is the person in this country who does all the trade. He is the hoarder and profiteerer [*sic*] . . . It is all rot to say there are pogroms in Poland . . . It is all Jewish propaganda, in my opinion they are very dangerous people in these days and are at the bottom of all Bolshevism in Russia . . . a dishonest, unpatriotic crew' (a line that must reflect what Mellor hears from his aristocratic friends: to be fair, and almost despite himself, he recognises that the Left, Jewish or not, are willing to co-operate in the restoration of decent government).

Mellor's part in Poland came to an end after a few months in May 1920, just as the Polish-Bolshevik war was starting in earnest. The reason given by the Poles was that they could not afford the hard currency; more probably, they felt that they owed nothing to an England which refused to help their crusade in the Ukraine; and anyway Mellor himself cannot have been a popular figure as he tried to put order into the police force. It followed Russian lines – i.e. so badly paid that it resorted to bribery, and even mugging. Any speculator, trying to smuggle grain through town, could bribe a policeman to shut his eyes, and the result is that the poor starve, without rations, while the hotels do a wonderful trade in hot dinners going on for hours. Mellor's proposals, to dismiss most of the administration and to pay the constables more, is naturally not popular. The only public organisation which works is the fire brigade, and 'they are all Bolsheviks'. Mellor thinks, in fact that the Bolsheviks can only win if they invade Poland, and that the victorious Entente must give some help. Little help was sent: nevertheless, Pilsudski held the Bolsheviks in August 1920, and established Poland in generous frontiers. They were unmanageably large, but, just the same, reading his manuscript, I have a certain respect for the progress which the Poles made, despite wars and slump, between this period and 1939.

11 July 1987

TAKI

BIG BANG THEORY

After Beverly Hills, the Wiltshire countryside seemed more beautiful than ever. Like eating an apple after weeks of a steady candy diet. My new ancestral country seat is a rented cottage on a large estate, and I look onto a beautiful Palladian house from which I expect Don Giovanni to emerge any moment. Until last weekend Monsieur Jeffrey Bernard was helping to give my new cottage a lived-in atmosphere. Very successfully, I may add. There is nothing more boring than brand new chintzes, brand new carpets, and brand new curtains, especially in an old house. After three weeks of Jeff, however, the house was no longer boring. There were some very smart cigarette burns in the carpet, a really beautiful red wine mark on the sofa, the curtains had been adequately drenched by the rain, and there were enough vodka bottles around to keep a Cossack regiment happy. Jeff, needless to say, was nowhere to be found.

Strange man, my low life colleague. I couldn't help wondering about him while inspecting his shaving kit. I don't really go in for that sort of thing, but in my haste not to miss my flight I left most of my things behind. The first thing that struck me was that his kit contained no less than three shaving brushes and two large shaving tubes of the instant foam type. The markings on the tubes were foreign, mostly Spanish and Italian. There were no less than five different sun creams, with one, the Hawaian Tropic, which features a little nude girl on the outside, neatly scratched out. There was also a bedroom slipper (left foot) with the picture of the nude girl inside it. By the time I had finished looking at his 'toilette', I was too scared to look anywhere else. For all I know Jeff could be running a black-market suntan-oil operation right from my ancestral country cottage, or worse, indulging in black magic. The only thing that is obvious he's not doing is writing. His desk – mine rather –was as pristine as Beverly Hills.

On Sunday I woke up late and went for a long run. Then I sat down to read the Sunday papers and nearly threw up. There was that man Knightley writing about sex again in the *Sunday Times*, an exercise as useful as writing about snikasnaka, which for any of you still unfamiliar with this ancient art is Californian close gardening. If any of you missed it, here is a brief example: 'According to our survey, a typical Alliance woman will have had her period at about the same time as women from the other two parties.' Ye Gods, what a discovery. Upon reading it I flung myself on the bed and screamed out loud with frustration at not having thought of that before the ghastly Knightley. But let me give you another example: 'Alliance women enjoy 2.21 sexual acts a week, compared with 1.82 a week for Labour and 1.65 times for Conservatives. Alliance women and, surprisingly, Tory women enjoy sex more than Labour women.' That, needless to say, did not shock me at all. In fact I knew it before Knightley, although I must admit I thought that Alliance women did it 22.1 times per week, rather than 2.21. Ditto as far as the Tories are concerned. In both cases I had my period in the wrong place.

MORI to the point, however, is the fact that Tory and Alliance women enjoy it more than Labour ladies. And it's not surprising either. If I was a lady I certainly wouldn't enjoy making love with, say, Scargill or Livingstone, or that dreadful Welshman with red hair and freckles. But enough about sex, Knightley dreams, and MORI polls.

All that afternoon I wandered around the property looking for some Alliance women, but to no avail. I did run into a couple of Tory girls but they were both reluctant to raise the Tory average. I suppose it has a lot to do with the size of one's house. When I was still living in my grand ancestral seat I had no problems with the fair sex. That is probably why my estimates were so far out. Now that I live in a cottage I realise that my figures were inflated. Show me the house you live in and I'll tell you how many girls you'll have each week, says an ancient Greek proverb. No wonder that Jeff is nowhere to be found. When he last stayed with me at Bruern Abbey I had to call two heavies to evict him. I guess, like blondes and the rich, people with big houses have more fun.

12 May 1984

EMPEROR OF SLOUGH

Athens

'Phone for the fish-knives, Norman' is the only thing that comes to mind after three days and nights in the Big Olive. If Betjeman were here he would publicly apologise to Slough, a place that seems like pre-war Dresden by comparison. The expensive restaurants and night-clubs are jammed with a new type of Greek, the Papandreou Philistine, a humanoid that is more often than not mistaken for a rock star when travelling abroad. The last time I saw so many hirsute and repulsive-looking people was when I attended my first – and last – pop concert back in 1975, guest of one Bianca Jagger, now better known as the world's oldest up-and-coming starlet.

Mind you, I feel lucky to be here. Last Sunday the Olive Republic got hit by the kind of storm that left Hyde Park treeless not so long ago, and I found myself in the middle of it – right above the Acropolis, to be exact. To say that the aeroplane resembled a Greek Orthodox church at Easter would be a gross understatement. Never have I seen so many pray so hard and for so long. Some Greeks even stopped smoking while begging the Almighty to save them in order to continue to screw their fellow man.

Greeks are notorious for thinking out loud, and they were louder than usual last Sunday. The lady sitting behind me, however, was an exception. She cried softly throughout, while repeating, 'The pilot can't see, the pilot can't see, we're finished, I tell you, we're finished.' I finally took pity on her – well, perhaps she was unnerving me – and told her that thank God the pilot couldn't see, because we were going in on instruments, and that instruments did not need to see. 'Ah, ah, don't say such things, don't say such things,' was her reply.

Things got worse after we landed. My two karate boys, Dimitri and Elias Kazakeas, were waiting for me, and as we left the airport I got the strange feeling that I was entering a war zone. In fact the last time I had had that particular feeling was while landing in Da Nang in the spring of 1972, just after 40 divisions of the NVA had crossed the DMZ. The Big Olive looked like Athens in the winter of 1944, the only lights being those of a few cars. It was soon explained to me that when it rains the city's electricity system goes on the blink, as the funds that were allocated for it went for the most part into the pockets of the officials who allocated them. The funds for the overhaul of the system ditto, and so on. As Aristotle said, par for the course.

Aristotle, needless to say, would have been put on trial by the present government because he would have shouted out loud at the antics of the master clown of Europe. Andreas the First continues to indulge in his various schemes of global design in order to keep a high profile, while dissatisfaction among his subjects is approaching a St Petersburg circa 1917 pitch. The same, however, is unfortunately happening as regards the opposition party. The conservatives are hopelessly split, a fact that Papandreou exploits to the hilt. The communists are even more obsolete than the Albanians, and are busy trying to out-Moscow Moscow. Which means that the poor old Olive Republic is going to get five more years of imperial rule from Andreas, a master at outmanoeuvring his sluggish opponents in political matters.

Here are a few examples of Andreas's Houdini-like antics: on the sluggish and stagnant economy, Andreas declared that Greece in 1988 would have an economic development equivalent to that of . . . West Germany. No figures were given and the government-controlled media didn't ask for any. On the pollution that is literally killing the four million inhabitants of the Big Olive, a spokesman for the emperor called a press conference and announced that a special police squad would be responsible for the prevention of atmospheric pollution and that ten mobile units would be assigned to check car exhaust fumes. The spokesman also said that great plans were afoot to build public garages and parking lots. The fact that the régime has been in power for seven whole years and the first brick for a public garage has yet to be laid made no difference. The media applauded, as did the ten units which will check the cars of the various ministers to make sure they are in good running order.

What is definite is that huge sums of public money will find themselves in private pockets, and that more and more

Papandreou Philistines will be breaking plates and dancing on the tables of my once favourite haunts. I guess it's no different in Eastern Europe, where the sons of ministers lord it over old families now employed as waiters. Which reminds me: back in 1951 I spent the summer working as a bus boy in a Connecticut resort. Next time I hope I make it at least as a maitre d'.

20 February 1988

SALLY VINCENT

THE MEN ON THE CLAPHAM OMNIBUS

Saturday evenings at 52 Clapham High St, SW4. 31 Oct. 'Spotlight on Aircraft Industry'. Open discussion. 7.30. Buffet at 9.30. The Socialist Party of Great Britain. (*New Statesman.*)

The impossible hood of the railway bridge and black girls in pastel dresses going to dances. Great hangars of stores offering items for the home at high prices; chipped crockery with odd lids, jelly-mould suites and knocked-down ironing boards, second-hand sideboards and biscuit barrels and plastic buckets. Clapham High Street has accepted no favours.

Whoever is inside number fifty-two is going to change all this. Revolutionaries have their meetings in this box, members of the Socialist Party of Great Britain. They are against a lot of things. Against capitalism, against frontiers, against all other political parties, against all leadership, against racialism and against war. They believe in happiness and in the pursuit of happiness, rather as we did in the fifth form before we lost sight of the possibility that our little philosophies were right, or if not right then good, or if not good then at least innocent.

Between grey walls and beneath daylight strips chains are arranged as an audience to a red-clothed table accommodating a tape recorder, two glasses, a jug of water and a bell. Seven people are present and one man, perhaps because of his authoritative situation behind the table, perhaps because there is something in the way he handles his pipe and combs his hair that reminds of Harold Wilson, seems at once to be dominant. A young man with fierce eyes and an anorak is conversing with an older woman, she sitting twisted to face him because her chair is looking the other way. They are discussing advertising techniques, their voices raised so that their argument may be coherent to the rest of the assembly, which gives no sign of involvement.

'You decide,' he says, 'how much money you've got to spend. If you decide £20 you start from that and you make the best use of it. Then you decide the leaflet is going to be so big and it's going to be red.' OK.

'Now look, nobody in this country's worried about a ha'penny or a penny any more.' Certainly not.

'Now look, how many adults in Britain? Forty million? Thirty million?' They settle for twenty-five. They also settle for the suggestion that more than one adult tends to live in any one house at any one time.

'We find,' says the lady, crooked in her chair, 'wherever we go that nobody gives a straight answer to a straight question. From Land's End to John o'Groats it's the same. There are only about two hundred people in any area who are reasonably responsive.'

Three more people come in, settling themselves away from the others, but only on one side of the room, like the pieces in an exhausted chess game. They appear not to hear the conversation in progress. 'Capitalism works for us. It actually helps our propaganda to work because it makes people so unhappy.'

We have swollen to some fifteen souls, not counting three behind the table replacing the Harold Wilson gentleman who has retired to the back row.

Our chairman has a neat grey suit and a short-back-and-sides and he bids comrades and friends good evening. He introduces Comrade Ken who is going to talk for twenty minutes about the aircraft industry, a subject of great interest and information, not to mention controversy but most of all interest.

Comrade Ken wonders if we mind if he remains seated as he is a little weak in the knees and a young man in a maroon hand-knitted jumper starts the tape-recorder. Comrade Ken laments that he has only twenty minutes to describe for us just a few of the many interesting and informative aspects of the aircraft industry. A brief outline of its history, he promises, followed by a brief (alas for the restricting twenty minutes) word on the situation as it stands today.

A fellow with a football crowd face and a tartan scarf falls asleep, but Comrade Chairman is alert, nodding with infinite generosity when Comrade Ken's voice rises to the end of a sentence. A similarly warm-hearted man in the audience smiles whenever the phrase 'you know' is uttered, as though it was a great intimacy.

We learn that the pre-war aircraft industry was a simple business compared with the complexity and sophistication of the post-war industry. We learn that it takes longer to make an aircraft today than it did years ago. We hear about vertical take-off and variable geometry and a thousand intolerably boring and accurate facts about aeroplanes. An old man has placed himself in the front row, directly in front of Comrade Ken. Throughout the lecture, which lasts, despite apologies, far more than twenty minutes, he sits in enviable relaxation, the controls of his deaf-aid in his placidly lapped hands, an expression of sweet tolerance on his face. He has suffered the promise and the disappointment of Ramsay MacDonald and he still knows who his friends are.

At question time we realise nobody has been bored. Statements, thinly disguised as questions, spring to all the Comrades' lips. The dominant fellow at the back has to see to it that everybody gets a chance. Everybody knows something about aeroplanes and everybody wants to prove it.

Comrade Chairman thanks Comrade Ken and grieves again for the inappropriate time span, but the dominant Comrade has made his decision. A few words, he says. Capitalism has not been cursed, in fact, for all anyone might have gathered it might as well be an acceptable condition. The Socialist point of view has not been stressed. Flying is not a civilised and happy way to get from point A to point B. It is altogether nicer to traverse the Atlantic in the 'Queen Elizabeth' than to sit all cramped up in a jet and what is more the food is better. Furthermore it is better to go from London to Manchester in a train than to fly there. And still furthermore, all those jumbo-jets are coming in half-empty. The whole point is that the capitalists are wasting money on prestige projects instead of concerning themselves with human happiness. So there we go, and in case that's not enough we want you to know that a good Socialist system could produce a non-stick frying pan without sending men to the moon.

Somebody who has frowned all evening selects a match from his box and circulates it in his left ear. Mr Chairman announces buffet time unless someone has something pressing. Someone has. If only the customs would let the people through there would be less congestion in the air, less congestion all round. They could let the people through and keep moving like on the buses. No, no, it's the congestion of the traffic in the air. Yes, but if the customs let you through . . . A cup of tea, Comrades. And many thanks for the £2 9s 6d raised in the collection.

The comrades drift singly behind a serge curtain, from which they emerge holding a cup of tea and a plate with sandwich, mince tart and slice of sponge. They replace themselves in the seats they have vacated, each with his own space around himself. Not a chair is disturbed. The comrades contort themselves to face each other but never, ever, move a piece of furniture.

'Even the old Duke of Edinburgh is complaining about the noise.'

'He'd have to, wouldn't he, living at Windsor Castle just where they come over.'

'They used to be able to get away from the workers, but they can't any more.'

'We're all in it together now.'

7 November 1970

AUBERON WAUGH

A MAN AND HIS DOG

Of all the letters which have appeared in *The Times* since the Home Policy Committee of the Labour Party proposed that Labour's election manifesto should promise to forbid blood sports, one of the most eloquent came from Lord Ferrier. He is a seventy-eight-year-old former Bombay hand who accepted a life peerage in 1958, before life peers became the figures of fun they are today:

> Sir, I imagine that I am not alone in being somewhat surprised that letters and articles about the current threat to hunting and shooting contain so few references to the age-old relationship between man and his dog . . .

There is something unbearably poignant at the thought of Lord Ferrier, seventy-eight, being alone, but I must admit that it had not occurred to me to be surprised that so few people in the great blood sports debate had referred to the age-old relationship between man and his dog.

Lord Ferrier continues:

> No one who has not at least whipped in to hounds or brought up a dog as his companion in venery can know of the skills and emotions entailed.

Those of use who have whipped in to hounds, must, indeed, form a tiny proportion of the total adult population. When he speaks of bringing up a dog as his companion in venery he is, of couse, using 'venery' in its dignified if archaic meaning of hunting. So far as its more usual meaning – the pursuit of sexual pleasure – is concerned, I know of only one man who was ever given to this practice, the controversial C. R. M. F. Cruttwell, one time Principal of Hertford College, Oxford, but he died, unmarried and insane, in 1941, and is in no position to tell us of the skills and emotions entailed. It was from this unfortunate man that the word 'Crutwellism' was coined to describe the abominable vice of sodomy with a dog, but his peculiarity dated from experiences in the trenches of the Great War, and I cannot believe it is really very prevalent today. I have been told that a carpet of his is preserved in Hertford College, covered with indescribable stains, but if he is remembered at all in the world outside, it is usually with pity. Nobody spares a thought for his dogs.

Perhaps it is time we did. But that is not the point Lord Ferrier is making. He asks us to regard this age-old relationship in the perspective of the national economy:

> Incidentally, the breeding and training of hounds and gun-dogs involves a considerable measure of employment and contributes to exports to the country's balance of payments – over and above sport, itself.
> I am, Sir, yours etc.
> FERRIER
> House of Lords

Unfortunately, I don't know the exact proportion of our national export effort which is taken up in the breeding and training of hounds and gun-dogs, so I am in no position to join the economic aspect of the debate. But I worked for many years as a political correspondent in and around Westminster, so I may be in a position to assess the political weight which is likely to attach to his Lordship's argument. And that, of course, is precisely nil. I wonder if economic arguments are really the ones most likely to be effective.

If the blood sports proposal is accepted by Labour's National Executive, and if Labour wins the election – neither eventuality seems impossible – tens of thousands of people in this country are going to find their lives in ruins. They will have nothing else to live for. This may seem an exaggerated statement, even an absurd one, but it happens to be the truth. Jorrocks is speaking for the entire hunting fraternity when he remarks: ''Unting is all that's worth living for – all time is lost wot is not spent in 'unting – it is like the hair we breathe – if we have it not we die . . .'

The tragedy is that hunting people seem too shy, or too well-mannered, or too inarticulate, to convey the enormity of their loss. They assume that the 'don't-knows' will be influenced by piffling considerations like profit and loss on the external trading account, by valid but strangely unconvincing arguments about conservation of the countryside, by preposterous and contradictory claims about the survival of foxes on the one hand – apparently they have entirely disappeared from areas where they are not hunted – and humane control of their numbers on the other, as if foxes would take over the country if man relented from his struggle.

Mr Vic Finlayson, the Labour prospective parliamentary candidate for Devizes, describes the issue as being one of town versus country rather than left versus right, and in an important sense this is true. Hunting people, in their dismay, see Labour's proposals almost entirely in terms of the class war, and this interpretation may be useful in attracting the support of non-hunting right-wingers, but they have got it wrong. No doubt there are elements of class vindictiveness, envy and simple sadism in the political decision, but the decision also reflects a widespread and entirely non-political horror of killing animals. This was well expressed by another correspondent, Mr Alan Long, of the Vegetarian Society of the United Kingdom, who wrote of 'the cardinal doctrine of liberty, to live and let live'.

It would be comforting to suppose that these confused notions flourish only in the town, while the country is single-minded in its loyalty to the hunting fraternity. But I am terribly afraid Mr Finlayson has made an electoral miscalculation, ignoring the extent to which the countryside has been infiltrated by retired folk who come to batten off its welfare services and sit around in their custom-built bungalows grinding their false teeth at poor, caged budgerigars as they await alike th'inevitable hour. If Mr Finlayson were a less honourable or admirable man, Devizes is exactly the sort of constituency where Labour's proposals on hunting might have made a difference. In October 1974, it divided 42 per cent Tory, 30 per cent Labour, 27 per cent Liberal. If one allows for the fact that people with anti-hunting views often hold them very strongly indeed, and retired folk who would otherwise vote Conservative often become obsessive about such things, and if one allows also for that very large Liberal vote which is now up for grabs, I would not be in the least surprised if there were three thousand votes going begging on the issue. The same would be true of Taunton and many, if not most, of the agricultural West Country constituencies now swamped in the geriatric invasion.

Which rather takes us back to contemplating the age-old relationship between man and his dog and it is here, I feel, that the answer may lie – as well as in the newer relationship developing between man and his budgerigar. However one looks at it, the general election is unlikely to be won or lost on the blood sports issue, and there is a decent chance that Mrs Thatcher will win. It is tempting to plan elaborate revenges in the class war – she could respond to popular feeling against football hooligans by banning all football matches and converting the pools to a National Lottery. But I fear that the Tories lack my fine aggressive spirit – and indeed, the fine aggressive spirit of the Labour left.

There is no chance of converting animal-lovers to the cause of blood sports, and the only hope is to shut them up and put them on the defensive. Urban dog-owners are already the focus of considerable resentment, and urban dog-shit contributes nothing towards badly needed exports. Let us propose a £50 dog licence for non-working dogs. Next, to add that disconcerting element of moral outrage to our compaign, let us crusade against the sale and ownership of caged birds.

> A purple Budgie in a Cage
> Puts all Heaven in a Rage.

But it may need a rabies epidemic to remind us that this partnership between a man and his dog has never been an equal one.

24 June 1978

WINE AND THE PRESS COUNCIL

Next month marks the launching of the *Spectator* Wine Club with a monthly wine column promoting its wares which will be written by myself. Also next month, on 28 October, Gollancz publishes an English version of Louis Forest's famous *Monseigneur Le Vin* of 1927 under the title *Wine Album* and at the price of £6.95. The text offers a wine vocabulary – 'engaging'; 'seductive'; 'amorous'; 'voluptuous'; 'shameless'; 'plebeian'; 'a lout' – which I, as a wine writer, almost certainly won't find useful at all.

This problem of trying to describe a taste was one which I tackled quite squarely – or so I thought – in the first of a series of wine columns which I have been writing for some time in *Tatler* magazine under the pseudonym of Crispin de St Crispian. Although the original inspiration for Mr de St Crispian came from Bertram Wooster's famous article on *What the Well Dressed Young Man is Wearing* in a similar publication, Crispin rather ran away with the part to emerge as a somewhat exaggerated sort of fellow. If *Spectator* readers will forgive me for importing this improbable character into their own chaste pages, I will quote the relevant passage. My reasons will soon be clear:

'. . . Prose writing which tries to describe a taste can become vulgar and even rather disgusting, when it resorts to metaphor and allusion. The art of the business is to choose references which become more and more preposterous and inappropriate as the second and third bottles are produced.

'Comparisons may be made with music, or motor cars, or favourite football players, the sexual performance of famous women or shared acquaintances, but it must be extravagant, histrionic and absurd. It simply will not do, when given a wine which costs more than £6 or £7 a bottle, to say it is jolly good or absolutely delicious. That is not playing the game . . . People who have skimped on wine should be made to suffer for it. Their wine should be compared to a creaky old woman's bicycle in a Merseyside cul-de-sac, a bunch of dead chrysanthemums on the grave of a still-born West Indian baby . . .'

Some time after this had appeared, I received a letter which purported to come from a midwife in Camden. She said that her experience with still-born West Indian babies made this reference to them in a wine article both tasteless and offensive, and that she proposed to complain to the Press Council. I do not remember whether I answered her letter or not – I hope not, because at this stage I was half-persuaded that it was a practical joke by Patrick Marnham. Those who know Marnham have to suffer these little jokes from time to time. It seemed most unlikely that Camden midwives would read the *Tatler*, unless in their dentist's waiting room. Nobody's judgment is at its best when suffering from a toothache. Best thing was to get rid of the letter and forget about it all.

But I can quite see that the reference might indeed have stirred unhappy thoughts among West Indian mothers who had suffered a still birth and among those public functionaries whose business it is to cope with such tragedies. No use to argue that for such people the image would be even more relevant, more poignant. The plain truth is that writers cannot hope to cater for everybody's private grief or anxiety. Wodehouse's famous description of the prize-giving at Market Snodsbury Grammar School would not be suitable reading at the funeral service of an alcoholic, but that is not criticism of Wodehouse. Similarly, I cannot think of a single thing I write which would be suitable for the Health and Social Welfare workers on Camden Borough Council. There are plenty of magazines which cater almost exclusively for their gloomy preoccupations. I do not read *New Society* or *New Statesman* or *New Departures in Modern Verse*; why on earth should they read *Tatler*?

There the matter rested until this week when a sheaf of papers arrived through the post from the Press Council. Ms Somebody-or-other's complaint had been taken up by no less a person than the Camden Community Relations Officer on behalf of the Camden Committee for Community Relations, Mr Christopher ('Chris') Adamson. At the same time as complaining to the Press Council, Mr Adamson issued a press statement, published in part in the *Hampstead and Highgate Express* on 23 July, describing my article as 'totally distasteful': 'I consider at best that the sentence is in extremely bad taste, and at worst could well be considered racist,' says Chris, explaining, 'by the addition of the reference to a "stillborn, West Indian baby" he implies that another baby (perhaps a white one) would not be so bad.'

Oh dear, oh dear, I have great admiration for the Press Council, and strongly believe one should always keep a-hold of nurse for fear of finding something worse. Under normal circumstances I would not dream of discussing a complaint against me until it had been heard, but I fancy that when the complainant issues statements to the press putting his point of view in advance then he has forfeited his right to that particular courtesy. Among the sheaf of documents, I see a reply to Mr Adamson's original complaint from Ms Tina Brown, the elegant and energetic Editor-in-Chief of *Tatler*. She wrote:

'There is, in my view, no question of "racism". It is quite clear that Mr Waugh is using the illustration to which you object, as with the reference to the old woman's bicycle, to evoke pity. He is comparing poor wine to something sad and depressing. That is all.'

Ms Brown, bless her, is obviously used to dealing with these people. My ignorance of the Camden Borough race industry and its strange theology is almost total, living as I do in West Somerset. Surely a white racist would be *more* appalled by the thought of a little white corpse? 'West Indian', applied to wine, suggests a hint of curried mangoes, with chillies and other spices – none of them flavours I would normally look for in wine. Does this make me racist?

The truth is I neither know nor care. But the suggestion that Camden's Community Relations Officer is a suitable person to pass judgment on matters of literary taste strikes me as a bizarre one. I wonder what he and his Committee make of the following, and whether they would allow it to be chanted at public performances in the Borough:

> Liver of blaspheming Jew
> Gall of goat and slips of yew
> Silver'd in the moon's eclipse
> Nose of Turk and Tartar's lips
> Finger of birth-strangled babe
> Ditch-deliver'd by a drab
> Make the gruel thick and slab.

Let the Press Council decide. I see that I am invited to attend, although no date is fixed for the hearing. If I am in England, I shall certainly do so. Perhaps they will let me wear a false moustache in my Crispin de St Crispian *persona*. If they also allow me, I shall take along some bottles of really unpleasant wine, so they can judge for themselves whether my comments are justified or not. The bottle which inspired the 'dead chrysanthemums' image was served by a cousin (quite a bit richer than I am) in North Devon, but he has since improved the quality of his wine – possibly as a result of my comments. I have plenty of bottles which are even worse. One, sent to me by the Hungerford Wine Company at £3.11½p, is a Californian Alicante Bouschet from the Angelo Papagni vineyards. Its taste of kerosene, scorched buildings and other more biological smells conjures only one image in my mind, that of a bombed hospital in the Arab quarters of Beirut. Can this get by the Camden community relations literary panel? Or the Camden Borough midwives' circle? Or any of the busy-bodies and trouble-makers, the boring, bossy, ignorant, humourless cows of both sexes on the Camden Borough payroll? Let the Press Council Wine Panel decide.

25 September 1982

I blame these violent sagas.

MR WU IS 60

Londoners were deprived of the *Daily Telegraph* on three days of last week, as the result of an industrial dispute about the movement of some machinery. In West Somerset, for some reason, we saw the newspaper only on Monday and Tuesday. The other four days had me earnestly reading the *Times*, a newspaper which arrives with the regularity of clockwork these days but is seldom opened.

Why do we go on taking it? Soon, if reports of its gigantic

losses this year are confirmed, we may be spared the embarrassment of having to explain, although I have a sick feeling that
some organisation like the Arts Council will step in and save it
for the nation yet again. One reason may be snobbery or class
deference. Is not the present editor a first cousin once removed
of the Princess of Wales? Perhaps this explains why it now
shows the Royal arms not only on the masthead and above the
Court Circular, but also above the almost unreadable Times
Diary facing the leader page, and even to advertise the
completely unreadable Saturday Leisure Supplement on page
one. It now uses the Royal arms as a sort of trade mark, as if the
newspaper held a Royal warrant. I am almost sure it doesn't,
and suspect that Clause 68 of the Trade Marks Act 1905 has
some pretty austere things to say about tradesmen who use the
Royal arms in this way without authority. Whether Douglas-
Home risks being beheaded or just a stiff prison sentence, it
certainly will not be the first time that someone has allowed a
Royal connection to go to his head.

The boredom of the new *Times* is, I suspect, deliberate, as if
there was some moral or historical obligation to be boring in
response to the pressures of the age. My real complaint, having
thought about the matter, is not so much that it is boring, but
that it fails to carry conviction in its efforts to be boring. It is
like some raw adolescent who has once met a captain in the Pay
Corps and is trying to pass himself off as a retired Indian Army
colonel from Poona.

The classic example of boredom overkill in Saturday's
newspaper was the Parliamentary report. Spread across three
columns on page four we read the memorable headline:
'Revised welfare codes for pigs and cattle.' Thirty-nine column
inches devoted to a Commons debate on the report of the Select
Committee on Animal Welfare in Poultry, Pig and Veal Calf
Production were decorated by a studio photograph of the
Conservative Member for Plymouth Drake, Miss Janet Fooks,
who had contributed the thought that very small cages for
battery-reared calves were objectionable; but she was prepared
to accept a little longer than five years for phasing them out.

The main news story, on a day when most papers led on the
Helen Smith inquest, was Mr Lawson's failure to sell his British
Oil shares to the public. That, I suppose, is fair enough. But the

second news story was headed: 'China replaces defence and foreign ministers', splashed across two columns at the top of the front page. Forty-one column inches of news-space and 22 column inches of editorial opinion were then devoted to saying that not too much importance should be attached to this development, by which Mr Geng Biao was replaced by Mr Zhang Aiping, and Mr Wu Xiuquan replaced Mr Huang Hua.

The first leader – on French Exocets to Argentina – was reasonably concise and intelligent, but the second one, on Sino-Soviet relations, seemed such obvious waffle as to raise the question whether it was satirically intended. And this, it seems to me, is the crux. Let us examine the news item more closely.

I do not suppose that more than a hundredth of one per cent of the *Times*'s readership had the faintest idea who was the Chinese defence minister (answer – Mr Geng Biao) before learning that they should not be too alarmed at his replacement by Mr Zhang Aiping. But the whole act depends on maintaining the pretence that *Times* readers knew and cared who the Chinese defence minister was. Immediately afterwards we learned that Mr Zhang Wenjin will soon be appointed ambassador to America. The story continues:

'Mr Huang's successor has a long history of service in the Communist Youth League ... His appointment is seen as reflecting his close relations with Mr Hu Yaobang, the new Secretary General of the Communist Party ... Mr Wu is 60. Mr Zhang, aged 72, is a veteran revolutionary ...'

Anybody who has got this far will suppose that Mr Zhang, aged 72, is Mr Zhang Wenjin, the projected ambassador last referred to. In fact, it refers to the first Mr Zhang Aiping, who has dropped out of the story 40 lines back. But who the hell is Mr Wu? Is this perhaps a misprint for Mr Hu, the new Secretary General of the Communist Party, who might easily be 60? No, if you read 45 lines back, past five other Chinese names, you will find it refers to Mr Huang's successor, Mr Wu Xiuquan.

My reason for drawing attention to this confusion of the two Zhangs and muddling of Mr Wu (who is 60) with Mr Hu (age undisclosed) is to suggest that nobody at the *Times* really supposed the story would be read. They are just going through the motions of producing a serious newspaper, a journal of record. Their concentration is not on what they are saying, but on the fact that they are saying it. As I suggest, they are simply acting a part. There is no satirical intention but a boredom with the part which expresses itself in the tendency of bad acting to slip into parody and burlesque.

So much for the news side. Let us look at the features, obviously intended as a leavening. The main feature article was what might, I suppose, be called a 'think piece' by Nicholas Fairbairn, the former Solicitor-General for Scotland who used to list 'making love' among his recreations in *Who's Who*. His article, called 'What the public need not know', complains about press interest in the private lives of public people, and also about the 'tone of moral disapproval' in press comment on Prince Andrew's adventures with Koo Stark (I did not notice any moral disapproval). He proceeds:

'There is much to be said for the law being changed, so that no comment may be made on the private life of anyone without his or her consent, unless it emerges from criminal pro-ceedings.'

Yes, well, that is a fine, pompous bloody fool's opinion and there is no earthly reason why it should not be freely expressed in a fine, pompous bloody fool's newspaper. No doubt it struck a chord in many breasts. Mr Fairbairn continues in the same vein:

'It is time that press hounding of those in public life ceased. Scandal may be good copy, but it adds nothing to the integrity of our institutions.'

As a penultimate sentence, that is grand. But then he has to destroy his whole argument with his last, parting shot:

'I do not think they [the institutions] were any worse, indeed I think they were probably much better, when those who ruled us were known and seen to have healthy sexual liasions with many mistresses and lovers.'

Which is precisely what press hounding achieves. Mr Fairbairn here reveals himself as healthy sexual liaiser, quite happy to be known as such provided comment is approving. He is an ordinary bore acting the part of a pompous bore. And that is the trouble with the *Times*.

There is no space to enlarge on two other horrors in Saturday's newspaper – the 'guided tour of the best of modern building in the City of London' or the full-page shopping guide to Hong Kong. My point is that if this silly, boring, bogus travesty of a newspaper survives, and an intelligent, professional one like the *Daily Telegraph* goes to the wall, it can only be a sign that the country is doomed. Poseurs and twerps will have triumphed not only in politics, where they have always been strong, but also in the presentation and interpretation of political events – and that is much more serious.

17 November 1982.

VALUABLE WOGGLE MYSTERY

On Friday of last week I received a letter asking me whether I would be prepared to repeat my subscription of last year to the Combe Florey branch of the Taunton Constituency Conservative Party. After long and earnest deliberation, I decided to send £9.50 this year, keeping back 50p in protest against the various unsatisfactory aspects of the present administration. Chief among these, as nobody will be surprised to hear, was my sorrow at Mrs Thatcher's increasingly pointed refusal to grant Sir Peregrine Worsthorne the knighthood which is already his by popular acclaim. No doubt many, if not most, Conservative supporters will feel tempted to do the same. But even if the Conservative Party finds its income seriously reduced can we be sure that Mrs Thatcher's admirers will draw the right conclusion, or that Mrs Thatcher will act on it if they do?

When I mentioned to someone who is high in Conservative councils a few weeks ago that I rather admired Mrs Thatcher for the way she was able to withstand the burning hatred of such a large part of the population – almost anywhere one goes north of the Trent she is seen as an ogress – he replied that he doubted whether she was even aware of their feelings.

She can scarcely be completely unaware of them after her recent tour of the North, when she and her husband were pelted with eggs, flour and paint in nearly every borough and market town of Lancashire. Perhaps she attributed it to the activities of a small group of unrepresentative extremists. If so, she is quite simply wrong. Those eggs represented the gut feeling of the entire industrial and post-industrial north about Mrs Thatcher. Anybody who doubts it should go there and find out for himself. The people up there attribute all their misfortunes and shortcomings to Mrs Thatcher's malice. One can waste hours of time, as I have done, trying to persuade them that they are unemployable, or pointing out that they are unbelievably well off, their unemployment benefits and other social security hand-outs more valuable than the wages of a fully employed skilled worker 30 years ago. They remain convinced that they are the victims of unfair discrimination, and they accordingly hate Mrs Thatcher with the sort of passion which Poles reserve for whoever is the top man in Russia.

Quite possibly no one could convince her of this. But she must worry a little about her reception in Lancashire. More than any other part of the country – more even, I should say, than Bermondsey – Lancashire is Worsthorne territory. Is she aware, for instance, that the Lord Lieutenant of Lancashire, Mr Simon Towneley, who has been a Justice of the Peace in the country for over 25 years, is also the brother of the slighted Sir Peregrine Worsthorne? Or that, in the words of that admirable book, *Debrett's Handbook of Distinguished People in British Life*: 'It is from the Worsthorne portion of the estates of the old recusant Towneley family that the subject of this entry derives his surname.'

I am not, of course, suggesting that Mr Towneley set the Lancashire mobs on Mrs Thatcher and her consort during their ill-advised journey into the heart of Worsthorne territory. But local loyalties run deep and fierce in those parts. Around Burnley, where Mr Towneley has his seat, and the neighbouring village of Worsthorne, there may well be a feeling of 'Bless the Squire and his relations', but it would be no exaggeration to say that there is strong pro-Worsthorne feeling throughout the whole of the north-east. From the village of Worsthorne (whose name Sir Peregrine's father, Colonel Alexander Koch de Gooreynd, himself assumed in 1923, reassuming his original one in 1937) it is but a jog up the A1 to Darlington, scene of next month's by-election.

It will be a crucial by-election, I suggest, not only for Worzel Gummidge but also for Mrs Thatcher and the Conservative Party. Various explanations have been put forward for the

Conservatives' lamentable performance in Bermondsey. Where Labour retained 44 per cent of its vote in the 1979 election (over 51 per cent if you count both Labour candidates), the Tory score was considerably under a quarter. It has been suggested that since the Conservative and Liberal candidates looked exactly the same, had the same name and made much the same sort of nondescript noises, there may have been confusion in the minds of the electors, as well as tactical vote-switching. But to be a Conservative in Bermondsey, I would imagine, involves a more full-blooded commitment to Conservative philosophy than that, and I would not be at all surprised to learn that the defection of so many Conservative voters is explained by disenchantment with certain aspects of Mrs Thatcher's administration . . .

Like many people, I had supposed that Mrs Thatcher's obstinate refusal to honour this wise and good man might be explained by a suspicion of intellectuals generally, or violent disagreement with his ideas. Even I do not always find myself in complete agreement with everything he writes. But I do not think that opposition to Sir Peregrine's beautiful thoughts explains Mrs Thatcher's scurvy treatment of him.

Another explanation for Mrs Thatcher's extraordinary behaviour – and the field is getting thinner now – is that she knows something about him which we do not know. I confess that although I used to think I knew all that could reasonably or decently be known about this most unsecretive of men, I began to have doubts last week when he finished his interesting Notebook with a curious story about a friend of his:

Sorry mate, nothing about a soul.

'A friend of mine has just had a valuable tie ring stolen from the changing room of the Turf Club,' he wrote. 'Not for a moment does he suspect any of the old servants, all of whom are totally trustworthy . . . Surely it is a sign of something or other when the members of a gentlemen's club are thought to be less honest than the staff?'

A few people who read those words idly may have decided that a 'valuable tie ring' was a normal sort of thing for a gentleman to leave in the changing room of his club. But what on earth is it? When I was a Boy Scout, we wore a curious leather ring which kept a scarf or kerchief in place. It was called a 'woggle'. But these were objects of no value. What would a valuable woggle look like? Presumably it would be made of gold or platinum with diamonds or other precious stones encrusted in its surface, but I have never seen such a thing on any human neck, and very much doubt whether it would be of any use for keeping a tie in place.

Although not a member of the Turf Club myself – and with no ambitions to become one – I rather resent the suggestion by Sir Peregrine's friend that this valuable tie ring must have been stolen by one of the 'suspiciously raffish' new young members. It seems to say much more about the times in which we live that a gentlemen's club is prepared to let people wear jewelled woggles than that a member, finding such an object in the changing room, should decide to confiscate it. But the big question remains: what sort of people does Sir Peregrine choose as his friends?

After the Orpington by-election of 1962 many attributed the Liberal landslide to the fact that the Conservative candidate, Peter Goldman, was a Jew, just as Peter Tatchell attributes his failure as Labour candidate in Bermondsey to rumours about his sexual proclivities. In Bermondsey, as I say, the Conservative and Liberal candidates were indistinguishable. I prefer to explain the Orpington debacle by the fact that Harold Macmillan was one of a long line of Conservative prime ministers who neglected to honour Peregrine Gerard Worsthorne. They all come to sticky ends, sooner or later. Darlington will tell us if I am right – unless, of course, Mrs Thatcher is prepared to tell us what she knows about this man.

5 March 1983

RICHARD WEST

POMMY-BASHING

On a bus in Johannesburg one day this year, a girl who had been looking over my shoulder at the *Spectator*, indicated a headline and asked: 'Excuse me, what does "Anglophobia" mean?' When I explained that it meant fear or dislike of the English, she looked rather puzzled. This exchange came back to my mind when I read the recent anti-English or 'pom bashing' remarks by Australian politicians, and noticed the sullen scowls of their Test players on TV this week. A girl on a Sydney bus might not know the word "Anglophobia", but she would know the feeling all right.

Indeed Australia is the one country to which I have been where an Englishman can expect to be met with hostility as soon as he opens his mouth in a public place. 'They drink warm beer and bath only once a week' is the stock abuse shouted by Sydney cabbies at those who are slow starting up at the green light, for Poms are widely regarded as bad drivers. This anglophobia – which does not I think extend to the Scots, Welsh or Irish – derives from the old hostility to imperial rule, to which has been added a new dislike of immigrant shop stewards and other trade union militants.

It is no use the Englishman pointing out that Australia's native trade unionists need no instruction in bloody-mindedness, as one can see in Broken Hills, the old mining community now union governed. There is no consistency among 'pom-bashers'. One English journalist was knocked to the ground and cursed as a 'Pommy pooftah' for having ordered a dry sherry, yet Sydney teems with Australian homosexuals. The Poms are often roundly accused of 'coming over here and stealing our women'. We lose all ways.

Having said this, I must admit that most of the English people I met in Australia give little grounds for national pride and indeed seemed to justify 'pom bashing'. In Sydney, for instance, I met a young man who regaled me for some time with anti-Australian jokes and boastful accounts of the fights he had won against 'convicts'. He then revealed, without spotting the irony, that he had managed to emigrate in spite of having served two prison sentences because his local police force had hushed up his record in order to get him out of the country. (Australia normally will not accept convicted criminals.) In Perth I met an English girl whose father and mother had gone back home (after coming with a state-assisted passage) because they disliked Australian bread.

Amazement at my countrymen increased after having been tipped off by a TV reporter (himself an Englishman) concerning a certain pub in down-town Sydney, on Pitt Street as I remember. During the week it is an average, that is to say rather dreary, Australian pub frequented mostly by office workers but which, at the weekends is taken over by young English immigrants. Their average age was just over twenty. I went into the smarter downstairs bar, what we would call the saloon, and started to talk with a young man and his girl friend, whose families had lived in the west of London. They came here each Friday and Saturday night, they said, in order to get away from Australians and to talk about England with other English people. The things they talked about most, they told me, were the unfriendliness of the Australians, the gassy beer, the lack of discotheques, the lack of good football teams and the incomprehensible accents. Since these young people and their friends had most of them been brought up in Australia I was surprised by their insularity and still more surprised to be told that even the English did not mix with each other. In the bar we were in, they were all 'Southerners' from below the Trent; to meet the 'Northerners' I would have to go to the other bar at street level.

In the public or 'Northerners' bar I met a boy of about eighteen whose parents had come out from Bradford when he was seven. He told me he did not enjoy Australia and indeed he still spoke with a Yorkshire accent, but life was all right as they had a nice 'unit' (Australian word for 'flat') and nice neighbours most of whom were from 'home'. 'You mean from the UK?' I prompted him. 'No, from Bradford and Leeds,' he corrected me, 'although there are some from Sheffield and even London.'

My surprise turned to bewilderment when this young man went on to explain that even within the 'Northers' bar there was no fraternisation between the Yorkshiremen, who drank on one side of the room, and the Lancashiremen, who drank on the other. The manager of the pub, an Australian, told me that sometimes after a football match in England, involving Leeds or Manchester or one of the Northern towns, there was quite a lot of argument.

What is it the English immigrants miss in Australia? They have their cars, TV, scandalous newspapers, racing, cricket, alcohol and a tolerant tradition of letting workers take 'sickies' or days off on Monday. For the Greek and Italian immigrants it is a different matter; they must learn a new language and way of life, which many find uncongenial. A Greek barber complained to me for example: 'In Greece, on Sunday, man puts on dark suit, goes to cafe, drinks coffee, talks with friends, family. Meets everyone. Laughs. Here in Australia, on Sunday, man stays at home. Wears shorts. Mows lawn. Drinks beer. Meets nobody. Does not laugh.' Australian suburban life makes no appeal to gregarious South Europeans but is not markedly different from life in an English suburb.

The mutual hostility of the Australians and the English has been put down to various economic and sociological causes, some of them no doubt valid, but there is also a quite irrational and instinctive dislike. Each people gets the other's goat. The old hostility between the two cricket teams, which blazed during the 'body-line' argument in the Thirties, was rekindled three years ago by the 'bouncer' dispute and still further inflamed this year by Kerry Packer's threat to the Test Series. Crass, bullying Packer, as seen on British TV, might serve as a caricature of his nation in British eyes. It now appears that the first result of his enterprise has been to destroy first the morale and then the competence of the very Australian team he has tried to buy. The resulting English triumphs and jubilation have irked the Australians and may be responsible for the outbursts of 'pommy-bashing'.

20 August 1977

A. N. WILSON

GUARDIAN OF THE WORD-HOARD

A supplement to the Oxford English Dictionary Volume III,
O-Scz Edited by R. W. Burchfield (Oxford £55)

Sufferers from night-melancholy and insomnia should console
themselves by thinking about New Zealand, and the bland
winds which waft over Wellington and Auckland. I have never
been there, and nor do I wish to, for I believe everything about
it to be excellent, and it would be sad to have one's illusions
shattered. They have Maoris, short stories (Dan Davin,
Katherine Mansfield), cheap butter, superb lamb and the only
unimpeachably heterosexual Anglican theological college on
the planet. When Great Britain stood alone against the world
after the Galtieri Raid, it was the Prime Minister of New
Zealand who was the first to offer support to Our Boys. And as
if all this were not enough, they have also provided us with
some of our most distinguished philologists.

In the field of phonology (sound-change) the world knows
no equal to Eric Dobson, who has recently retired as a
Professor of English Language at Oxford. Anything unknown
to Professor Dobson about vowel-sounds in the English
Language between 1500 and 1700 is not worth knowing. He has
also cracked the secrets surrounding the origin of that master-
piece of Middle English devotional prose, *Ancrene Wisse*. His is
one of the most original intelligences in post-war Oxford.
Needless to say, he is a New Zealander.

Phonology is a comparatively obscure science, so Professor
Dobson is only famous in his own field. Lexicography is
something which interests us all. And it is no surprise to
discover that the most distinguished lexicographer of modern
times, Dr Robert Burchfield, is also a New Zealander. He has
become something of a cult figure lately, and justly so. He gave
a brilliant interview with Bernard Levin, he appeared on *Call*

My Bluff, and on the radio programme *Tuesday Call* – what readers of the revised *Oxford Dictionary* would know as a phone-in (a word first recorded in the *New Statesman,* 1967).

For more than a quarter of a century, Dr Burchfield, assisted by a hard working team of experts, has been revising the great dictionary, and we have now reached Volume III, O-Scz. Those with ample bedside tables who tire of soothing their minds with thoughts of New Zealand sheep rations can now, for the cost of 1,100 cigarettes, peruse this magnificent and endlessly fascinating piece of modern archeology.

For the *Oxford English Dictionary* is an historical dictionary. Its task is to record usage, and to explain words in use. We have no French-style academy here, telling us what is, or is not, correct English. Infuriated letter-writers to *The Times* will tell us that *infer* does not 'mean the same' as *imply.* The *Oxford Dictionary* will merely relate that Milton used the two words indiscriminately. By turning its pages, we are not told that some words 'really mean' one thing rather than another; merely that they have been *used* in a particular sense.

It was in 1909 that Sir James Murray finished the letters O and P in the original dictionary. Sir William Craigie, working on Q and R, published his findings more or less contemporaneously, while Henry Bradley had started on S, getting as far as words beginning with Sc by 1911. In the years which have elapsed since, some inevitable lacunae, errors or omissions in these volumes have come to light. (They missed *salad-bowls* in Trollope). And the vocabulary of English has expanded at a rate of something like 450 words a year. Of these words, many are borrowed from foreign languages, some reflect the March of Mind, others were thought too coarse for inclusion first time round.

Dr Burchfield has followed the principles of his great predecessors. Lexicographers should not, in his view, be censors. The Jews objected to his inclusion of the offensive verb to *jew,* meaning to swindle. Doubtless, when he reaches W, there will be similar howls of protest about the verb to *welsh.* They both deserve to be included, not because they reflect the human language at its most edifying, but because they have been used. By the same token, he includes obscenities and Americanisms.

Dr Burchfield is recorded as believing that American and Standard English speech are diverging so fast that, within the space of a life-time or two, they will have become, effectively, different languages. This is almost certainly right. Any speaker of Standard English visiting New York today will find that he only understands about two-thirds of what is said to him; and that, for their part, the New Yorkers understand perhaps a quarter of the speech of an English visitor. We have gone far beyond a mere confusion over what is the first storey of a building, or what is meant by *trunk, purse, closet, fanny or bathroom*.

I doubt if it would be possible for the *Oxford Dictionary* to be comprehensive in its coverage of the American language, but the attempt made by this volume is most impressive. Addicts of modern American fiction can hardly afford to dispense with with this generous survey of yiddish, negro and pop vocabulary. Inevitably, one notices omissions. We find here *petting* ('the action of amatory caressing and fondling; non coital sexual activity') but not *parking*, in its sense frequently used in American True-Life Romance comics: 'to bring a motor vehicle to a stationary position for the purpose of amatory caressing' etc and so, by transference, 'to indulge in such caressing'.

I looked out for *Reno* vb. intrs. in this dictionary and was disappointed to find it was not included. Reno was the place where everyone used to go to get their divorce. 'To *Reno*' consequently came to mean to ditch one's spouse. Was it in the *Chicago Tribune* in 1936 that the famous headline appeared, announcing that Wallis Simpson had obtained a divorce in Ipswich? It would have been good to have it immortalised by Dr Burchfield: KING'S MOLL RENOS IN WOLSEY'S HOME TOWN.

Presumably *poppers* are of too recent vintage to have claimed the attention of the lexicographer. A recent article in *Time Out* described them as an aphrodisiac inhalant, said to cause cancer, and particularly popular with the *nancies and margeries*.

It was in 1850, incidentally, that someone first called them *poofs*; *poofter* was in a dictionary of Australian slang in 1910. The world had to wait until 1929, according to Dr Burchfield, for the first flowering of the *pansy*. (A much nicer word than *gay*: we would all read *Pansy News* and vote for *Pansy Rights*.

Much of the joy of reading *OED* derives from its qualities as an anthology. Under the aforementioned entry, for instance, there is the splendid sentence from Edmund Crispin's *Long Divorce* (1951): 'I'd want her to be walking out with a decent lad, not a pansy little foreign gramophone record'. It is much to be regretted that the ambiguity of the note pinned to the window-boxes by Sybil Colefax (*Please treat the pansies with respect*) disqualified it from entry here.

The evidence is drawn from a wide variety of sources: novels, newspapers, memoirs. The frequent recurrence of allusions to the work of Raymond Chandler, Eric Ambler, Ngaio Marsh, Agatha Christie and other masters of suspense doubtless reflects in part the tastes of the indefatigable Marghanita Laski, who has contributed over 30,000 of the quotations, a figure rivalled, among the voluntary assistants to Dr Burchfield, only by Mr Chowdhary-Best, who certainly deserves a mention. To them, and to all the other contributors named in the preface to this dictionary, the English-speaking world owes a huge debt.

But turning these pages is not all fun. The *Oxford Dictionary* is an admirable thing in itself, perhaps the most admirable thing this country has ever produced. But, in its patient record of the words we have been using for the last 60 years, it also tells the history of the world reflected in those words. And from that point of view, it is not a book to read late at night. On the same page that we read a quotation from the *Guardian* (1975) 'The higher education programme will contain a bias in favour of the *polytechnics*', we are also reminded of one of the nastiest inventions of science, *polystyrene*. One thinks of the rather batty, intelligent face of Dr Murray starting out from that velvet cap to the old photographers. It was a more innocent face than Dr Burchfield's. Murray knew nothing of *punk-rockers, Rastafarians, pricks or pseuds* (who made their first appearance in the *Spectator* in 1962). Murray probably ate boiled sheep's head for his supper. Dr Burchfield could, if he chose, have *pilau* and *pizzas, pop-corn* or *quiche*. Between courses, he could smoke *pot* or *read paperbacks*. Meanwhile, the human race could become (a thing unheard of to Dr Murray) *pissed* or *plastered*, join *quangoes*, send money to *Oxfam* or take part in a *phone-in*. The queers wear *polo-necks*, have *perms*, drink *Pepsi* (out of *polystyrene* cups), say *Okey-doke* and become *obsessional* about *Rubik's cubes*.

Has anything good happened since the demise of Murray? To judge from this book, very little. We must be thankful for small mercies, for *photocopiers, pony clubs*, the *Queen Mum* and the *old boy network*. And, of course, as always, good authors have invented locutions to the enrichment of our collective word-hoard. The strings of Betjeman's heart and his paramour's racket have gone *plung*! Little Noddy's car went *parp-parp*. They are crumbs of comfort to a generation plagued by *official secrets, phenobarbitone, pants rabbits* (American slang for body lice) and *o'nyong-nyong*. What's that? 'A mosquito-borne virus disease in East Africa': but we can be sure that it is only a matter of time before it reaches London.